CLOSER

—— *TO THE* ——

GROUND

An outdoor family's year on the water,
in the woods and at the table

DYLAN TOMINE

Foreword by Thomas McGuane
Illustrations by Nikki McClure

patagonia®
BOOKS

CLOSER TO THE GROUND

An outdoor family's year on the water,
in the woods, and at the table

Patagonia Books, an imprint of Patagonia Inc., publishes a select number
of titles on wilderness, wildlife, and outdoor sports that inspire
and restore a connection to the natural world.

FIRST EDITION

Illustrator Nikki McClure
Editor Susan Bell
Design & Production Good Apples
Project Manager Joyce Macias

PRESERVING OUR ENVIRONMENT
Patagonia Creative Services chose Cascade Enviro 100% post-consumer
recycled paper for the pages of this book, which was
printed in the United States.

Cover art Nikki McClure
Inset photo Dylan Tomine Collection

Library of Congress Control Number 2012934398
ISBN 978-1-938340-00-0

For Stacy, Skyla, and Weston

CONTENTS

AUTUMN

WINTER

FOREWORD
Thomas McGuane

Surely, *sustainable* must be among the most abused words in today's lifestyle vocabulary. For many, it imagines only two classes of people: the thoughtful and the stupid; the biodegradable versus the carbon footprint. For others, it suggests a mandate to live in a manner that, while not impossible, is uninviting to all but frowning zealots. Most writing on sustainability is aimed at those who enjoy being lectured, but the subject is too important to be framed so unattractively. People are baffled at having to choose between the gangplows of industrial farming and a two-man goat cheese operation. The real issue is that the condescension and finger pointing of too much environmental writing is not helping our most important cause.

Tomine's book is different. It does not castigate city dwellers and suburbanites for living in the dark. Dylan Tomine and his wife have lived that way themselves and found plenty to like about it. But they missed a greater connection with the earth – not so much disappearing from the grid as noticing weather, noticing seasons and animal migrations, tracking tides and enduring often hard physical contact in bringing part of their subsistence to hand. They wanted to do this without ignoring the intrusions and vicissitudes inherent to family life in the 21st century, and with the skyline of a major city in sight. It must be a satisfying life, because Tomine does not seem to feel called upon to cast aspersions on anyone else. How badly and greedily many of his countrymen live is for someone else to worry about.

The life he describes validates family values – but not the "family values" that we associate with the vassalage of organized religion. There's plenty of religion in this book, but it's embedded in the ceremonies of the Tomines, and in the wonder of a father and mother at the things their children do. It's the circuitry of a devoted family that absorbs the adults and makes the children feel important. They share the challenge and fulfillment offered by the natural world because they find, gather, and catch so much of it. Is this subsistence living? No. They also go to the store, whenever they feel like it. It's just that they shop with a little less urgency.

So many stories of this kind are about healing, but the Tomine family is not wounded. No sense looking into this book for food gathering as healing. These are buoyant people, and it's remarkable how absorbed the children are in foraging and how proud they are to eat and share the results. Nor has this life let them be easily bored, though they have seen plenty of bored children, made frantic and impatient by texting and social media.

This author is leading by example, and the quiet message is to learn to live with the things that really matter, the eternal things about the earth, and about each other.

McLeod, Montana

INTRODUCTION

Neck deep in salal and black huckleberry, covered with spiderwebs and dripping sweat, I stop to rest on an ancient windfall fir. It's too early for chanterelles to be showing in abundance, but I'm determined. So far, that determination has paid off with three tiny mushrooms and the creeping realization that I have no idea which way the trail lies. In short, I'm lost. Not catastrophically so – there are trails throughout the woods here, and I'm only about a mile from the house – but still, it makes you think. As I try to decide if that huge cedar stump looks familiar or not, I'm struck by a strange sense of nostalgia. Not a specific memory, but rather a feeling of what it was like to be a small kid in the woods searching for something I could eat.

Now that I think about it, I've always been a hunter-gatherer. Maybe it's some latent genetic code we all share, but for me, it goes back to my mom's "If you pick 'em, I'll bake it" blackberry pie policy. The thought of those fragrant pies, with their sweet-tart filling and savory lattice crust, was enough to send the neighborhood kids and me on nearly constant searches for the first, best, and last berries of the season. There was also a magnetic draw to poaching the neighbor's apples, pears, and raspberries; to the six-inch trout caught on the way to school and roasted over a twig fire; to the quail I sluiced with my trusty Daisy BB gun and triumphantly cooked for the family. That most of these activities were vaguely illegal only added to the allure. For a 10-year-old boy, it was delicious freedom knowing that I could find and eat my own wild food, even if I was limited to bicycle range and rarely left the confines of the small Oregon town where I grew up.

But as the years passed, new interests replaced childhood passions. Girls, sports, cars, school, and eventually, work, took priority, as they typically do with boys everywhere. Mucking around the woods or rivers became uncool and, more than that, detrimental to success at "real life" activities. The skinny kid riding his bike with a fly rod in one hand and half a dozen trout dangling from the handlebars discovers a larger world, and the purple-stained fingers of a hardcore berry picker fade.

There was a time when I found myself waking before dawn on winter mornings, riding an elevator down to the underground parking garage of my big-city high-rise apartment, driving through streets lit by neon to another underground parking lot, and riding yet another elevator up to my office. Nine hours later, in darkness again, I would reverse the process and end my day having never breathed a single breath of outside air. This was, and I suppose still is, considered "real life," by many of my colleagues.

During that time, I spent every weekend fishing and my allotted two-week vacation traveling to various outdoor destinations. But no matter how hard I tried, I could never quite shake the sensation of being a tourist in the activities that meant the most to me. It was unsatisfying, like coming into a theater in the middle of a movie and leaving before the end. Somehow, in pursuit of "real life" I had lost touch with the real world and its day-to-day rhythms of tide, weather, and season. It's one thing to look outside and say, "Better take an umbrella"; it's something else entirely when early autumn rain carries the significance of salmon migrating to river mouths and chanterelles emerging in the woods. It was this kind of meaning that I was missing.

But this is not a story of radical escape from city life, fraught with harrowing adventures of wilderness survival. We are neither yurt-dwelling back-to-the-landers nor flag-waving bunker separatists. We aren't off the grid, in the dark, or way out there. A failed crop or lousy fishing season simply means we'll go to the store a little more often. If I don't cut enough wood, we turn on the heat. We have electricity and plumbing, high-speed Internet, cable TV, DVD players, cell phones, laptops and all the rest of the usual suburban accoutrements. Most of our food still comes from the grocery store and we're not necessarily strangers at the mall or Costco.

In other words, I have nothing against the city. I can't even imagine living without it. Or, more precisely, I can't imagine living without its food: sushi, dim sum, proveletta, chile verde, laksa. Grinders from Grand Central Bakery. Various cured meats from Salumi. Handmade corn tortillas at El Puerco Lloron. A slice of pepperoni pizza from Pagliacci... These are just a few of the reasons that keep us from a true subsistence life in deep wilderness.

When it comes to living off the land, we are amateurs – recreationists, really – who've learned just enough to recognize how little we know. Luck still plays a major role in all our outdoor activities, with stumbles, setbacks, and miscalculations a familiar part of most days. Which is to say, if you're looking for any kind of expert, "how-to" advice, I would suggest you'll have much better luck elsewhere. In fact, the only subject I can reasonably claim to be an authority on is...well, it escapes me at the moment.

During our first years living together in Seattle, Stacy and I were dedicated urbanites, working, eating, and sleeping downtown and taking full advantage of everything the city had to offer. But gradually, we found ourselves shifting to a strange, part-time rural existence, motivated by a taste for wild foods we could only find in the country.

The life of a city-based dilettante hunter-gatherer, though, is not easy. Try parking a drift boat in a crowded underground garage or finding a place to dump crab guts in a high-rise apartment. Step into an elevator stinking of tidal mud and lugging a bucket of geoducks, and your neighbors press against the back wall with fear in their eyes.

Then we had Skyla. If we were already feeling the gravitational pull of a life more connected to the earth, our baby daughter was the catalyst. It wasn't long before we packed up and moved to this house in the woods on an island in Puget Sound, although that probably sounds more romantic than it really is. This particular island is merely a suburb of the big city we left, and many who live here commute daily by ferry to the high-rise office buildings we can see from our shores. Suburban sprawl, with its Nouveau Craftsman home clusters and manicured lawns, is rapidly consuming the old farms and open forest. But the Island has also managed to retain a deeply rooted sense of community, and at least for now, there's still plenty to keep us busy in the woods and on the water near home.

Clearly, our life here isn't about survival – at least not in the usual sense. For us, I think it's more about living and raising our children in a way that keeps us in touch with our surroundings. Our constant search for firewood, oysters, and mushrooms brings a heightened awareness to even the most mundane activities: Driving to the store for milk, we scan the roadside for windfall madrona trees, new tide flats, good places for chanterelles. Walking to the mailbox, we glance at the treetops for a reading on the wind. A dog-eared tide book hangs on the wall by the phone, and there's another in the car. The weather means more than just what shoes to wear or whether to pack an umbrella. This day-to-day, season-to-season awareness has become a vital part of our lives.

As parents, Stacy and I are just starting to understand how active participation in food gathering and production affects our children. When six-year-old Skyla and three-year-old Weston eat the tomatoes they grew, fish they caught, or berries they picked, we can see the pride that comes from contributing to family meals. When the kids serve these same foods to guests, their pride grows exponentially. The biggest surprise, though, is that our children have come to view healthy food – salmon, oysters, homegrown broccoli – as delicious treats. It could be their involvement in bringing these foods to the table, but it also might be the simple fact that fresh and wild foods taste better than what's available at the supermarket.

Another factor here is our search for ways to deal with the onslaught of electronic communication that seems to define modern life. It's not that I'm against technology. In fact, last year I learned text messaging so I could stay connected with our small fleet of anglers who share on-the-water reports. But not long ago, Stacy and I were at a barbecue hosted by friends with teenage kids. When I came inside to grab some fish for the grill, I saw two kids sitting at opposite ends of the couch, furiously texting away. It was sunny and warm outside, and here they were in a dark room, staring at cell phones. I asked with whom they were communicating, and without even glancing up, they pointed to each other. I couldn't help but feel this wasn't the future I wanted for my children. Perhaps in vain, Stacy and I hope that outdoor pursuits might balance the inevitable technological "advances" that are sure to be a part of their lives.

The process of finding or growing food with our kids provides learning opportunities for all of us. Of course, there are specific skills and knowledge, which accumulate over time, leading to better results and more consistent success. But there's something beyond that as well. Any student of Zen Buddhism can find valuable lessons while following a three-year-old as he moves through the woods searching for mushrooms. Everything – and I mean *everything* – along the way is significant, interesting, and fun. The actual picking of mushrooms is almost beside the point.

One of my false assumptions about outdoor activities with children was that achieving your stated goal – finding, catching, picking, harvesting – is crucial. I based this belief, in part, on my own goal-oriented approach to most things, but also on consistent input from friends, acquaintances, and media sources. I can't count the times I'd heard or read that *children have short attention spans, so if you want them to enjoy fishing, make sure they catch fish quickly and often.* It made sense and I bought into it. But on many occasions, I have found the opposite to be true.

For example, while salmon fishing last summer with the kids, we spent the day trolling, a technique where rods are placed in holders and left there until a fish is hooked. It increases the odds of catching fish by allowing you to cover a lot of water at specific depths. I figured we'd hook more salmon and the kids would be free to fidget, watch for wildlife, eat snacks, etc. We had a good day, but the kids seemed unusually subdued. I chalked it up to fatigue from our early start.

When it was time to quit, I cut off our fishing gear and ran the lines out behind the boat to untwist as we motored in. "Dad, can we hold the rods?" Skyla asked. I told her there weren't any hooks on the lines, that they wouldn't catch anything. "I know," she said, "but what we really like about fishing is holding the rods." Oh. I handed them each a rod with empty line trailing in our wake and both kids sparked to life – smiling, chattering, and cooking up fantastic make-believe fishing stories. I'm learning to redefine my understanding of the word "success."

People often ask about the financial benefits of wild food, and I always pause before answering. In light of recent economic conditions, foraging looks better and better all the time. In a 2008 survey of Washington State residents, a surprising percentage of our rural population said they actually looked forward to an economic collapse. Their reasoning? They could survive with hunting, fishing, and foraging skills. Hard times would validate their way of life. I admit, there was at least a little of this kind of thinking going on in our household as well. But the truth is, when you factor in time and equipment costs, it's probably cheaper to buy your beets or salmon at the store.

The value of eating from the land and sea, though, can't be calculated in simple fiscal terms. Salmon fishing, clam digging, gardening, and berry picking are all recreational activities that benefit our family, both on the dinner table and through the process of sharing time together outside. If we come out ahead in the capital expenditure column from time to time, we consider it a bonus.

Compared with other recreation I've enjoyed over the years, such as golf or catch-and-release fly-fishing, our current activities just seem to work better for the family. This wasn't an easy conclusion for me to reach, though. In fact, I came to it after years of releasing every fish I caught and working as a fishing guide and conservation advocate. To many of my friends in these circles, killing and eating fish you catch is considered something worse than sin.

But after a lot of thought, I don't believe the life we live conflicts with the ethics of conservation. I'm still deeply involved in conservation work and spend more than my share of time with a fly rod in hand, releasing the wild fish I catch. The fish we kill and eat today are only from hatchery origins or the rare healthy, sustainable wild stocks. Our firewood comes from windfall or trees felled for reasons other than burning. We grow our vegetables without pesticides or other chemicals. If anything, the process of harvesting food from nature has only increased our awareness of how human activity affects the environment. Are we "carbon neutral" or impact free? Not by a long shot. But we consciously do the best we can to minimize our footprints on the land and water.

Finally, there is this: Hunting, gathering, growing, fishing, processing, and cooking are all time consuming, labor intensive, and, at times, enormously frustrating. It would be a hell of a lot easier to just toss something in the microwave, sit on the couch, and flip on the TV. Add young children into the mix and I assure you, there will be times when parental forehead veins bulge and blood pressure soars. What always amazes me, though, are the small, unexpected moments of grace and beauty that rise from the chaos.

As I sit here, lost in the woods, the gathering dusk reminds me that I need to find the trail home. A few more chanterelles to go with the deer steaks I traded for last week wouldn't hurt, either. Now I'm pretty sure that cedar stump is the one that marks the mushroom bonanza we stumbled into last season. In which case, the trail lies just to the west. Or maybe it doesn't. But it occurs to me that this is really what it's all about: looking closely at the ground ahead, trying to find our place in the natural world.

Bainbridge Island, Washington

SPRING

LET'S GET THIS PARTY STARTED

Three minutes. Hardly more than the blink of an eye. But after a long, dark Puget Sound winter, the three additional minutes of sunlight we get each day now feel like salvation. Three minutes here, three minutes there...pretty soon you're talking real time. By the end of the month, our days will be nearly an hour and a half longer. Which means the morning school bus will no longer arrive in pitch-black night, the sun will clear the treetops to the south and we'll be able to see out into the woods during dinner. Small things, really, but like those three minutes, they add up.

There's no question winter here can take a chunk out of you. Not like the extreme cold of the upper Midwest or the round-the-clock darkness of Alaska might, but rather the opposite. Here, it's a general lack of severity – monotonous flat gray skies and the constant drip-drip of misty rain – that erodes the spirit. The short days limit outdoor activity and wet weather frequently reduces our inclination to venture out anyway. Time passes in a slow-motion slog through gloomy half-light. Inertia sets in.

Back in the days when successful foraging meant the difference between life and death, late winter was a time of great hunger as fat and food stores dwindled. If you didn't put up enough salal berry and suet logs, dried salmon, or deer jerky the year before, I imagine, it would have been a long, desperate wait for spring bracken shoots and the herring run. Today, our situation isn't nearly so dire, at least not in a physical sense. Yet I can feel our spirits growing thinner and weaker as the gray days and long nights accumulate.

We spend spring, summer, and fall trying to fill in the chunk winter takes from us. In a good year, with bountiful sunshine and blue skies, we fill it in and then some. But the surplus is never wasted. Our memories of long, warm, happy days are stored like fat cells to sustain us through the next winter. And now, with another winter drawing to a close, we're anxious to start replenishing our emotional reserves.

Those three little minutes mean something: We're over the hump. We're going to make it. Spring will, in fact, arrive.

There are other signs, too: a thick yellow dusting of alder and cedar pollen on car windshields; miraculous bright green buds along the spindly length of last year's lifeless brown raspberry canes; purple splashes of crocus pushing up through soggy earth. And perhaps most important, the moon lines up to pull seawater away from shore for the year's first daylight shellfish tides.

It might be a stretch to call February, with its heavy cloud cover, rain, and occasional snowfall, spring, but we don't care. Spring is *on the way*, which is what matters most. And like all creatures waking from hibernation, we're hungry.

There's a decent tide this afternoon, and I'm busy rounding up our clam and oyster gear. Or maybe that sounds too organized. What I'm really doing is thrashing through the garage, searching for items I put away in specific places last year so they'd be easy to find. Great plan. Only now I can't remember where those specific places are.

After much rummaging, four pairs of knee boots are lined up in the back of the car, along with a stack of five-gallon buckets, several mesh bags, and...I can't find the oyster knives. As I dig through more buckets and bins, Skyla comes out of the house wearing my rubber shucking gloves, a slender six-year-old girl with enormous, make-believe monster hands. She's clowning around, chasing three-year-old Weston, who shrieks in half-mock terror, trying to play along with big sister but unable to hide a touch of real fear. As they sprint past me on the gravel driveway, Skyla shouts over her shoulder, "Daddy, don't forget gloves for me and Weston!"

I finally locate the oyster knives, inexplicably stashed in a drawer full of screwdrivers, and grab a four-tined cultivator on my way back to the car. It has been dry all morning, but now that we're almost ready to go, it's raining. I head back into the house to track down our rain gear.

The kitchen is in turmoil. Stacy's packing the requisite piles of kid snacks and trying to match plastic containers with lids to hold our catch, while reminding the kids they need to go to the bathroom before we get in the car. We are not a well-oiled machine. In fact, pulling it all together for the first big family outing of the year has taken the better part of the morning. It briefly crosses my mind that I could have run out to the flats by myself, made a quick, efficient, solo harvest, and returned home by now.

Glen and Candace pull into the driveway right on time, and we run out to meet them. Between holidays, work, and the usual winter malaise, we haven't seen our old mainland friends in months. I laugh when Candace steps out of the car already clad in hip boots, but she's not kidding. She's *ready*. Hugs all around. While we stand in the rain catching up, I'm still going over my mental checklist. Then Gary and Kaia pull in with their boys, Finn and Beck. More hugs. More chaos. More happy, shrieking kids. I glance at my watch and give up on the mental checklist. Time to just start grabbing stuff and throwing it into the car. When the pile's big enough, I figure, we'll have what we need. We'll meet the Sweeneys there, we've packed enough food and equipment for an assault on Mt. Everest, and the tide, as everyone knows, waits for no man. We strap the kids in and our movable feast hits the road.

On the short drive to the beach, rain hammers the windshield in sheets and I start thinking I should have come up with a Plan B. Like bowling. On the hillsides there's a new reddish haze of emerging catkins in the alder thickets, and an optimistic cherry tree sheds a blizzard of pale pink blossoms in somebody's yard. A blast of wind rocks the car. Spring *is* coming, just not today.

Skyla and I discovered our oyster spot shortly after Weston was born, on a day when we both needed a break from the isolation and intensity – Stacy calls it "the baby cocoon" – enveloping our house. We jumped in the car and headed to a popular oyster beach, only to find it picked over and nearly barren. We walked along the water, talked and threw rocks, but couldn't quite escape feeling the disappointment of a fruitless foraging mission. I remembered seeing an old-timer earlier that morning pulling on knee boots at an inconspicuous, brushy little parking spot a couple of miles back, and thought we might check it out on the way home.

The guy was still there, returning to his car with a jar of shucked oysters and a bucket of steamer clams. When he saw us, he tried to hide his bounty, clearly unhappy that we'd found his secret spot. I pulled over and waved, and he ignored me, moving quickly now to avoid us. So I unleashed my secret weapon. It would take a hard heart to ignore a little girl in knee boots running up to see what you've caught. When Skyla told him of our failed venture, his defenses melted away, leaving a friendly grandfather happy to share the secrets of his no longer secret spot. He pointed out where the clams lived and told us that if we kept going around the corner, we'd find more oysters than we could imagine.

In the spirit of the old man's willingness to share – begrudging as it was – we've also shared this place with a few close friends. Out of respect for his initial secrecy, though, and the knowledge that "private" places on public land can be quickly decimated, we've limited our sharing to those who understand the value of such things. In the years since we first "discovered" this beach, the shellfish population has grown, and we seldom see anyone else there.

But this brings up some interesting questions. How much information should anyone share? Where is the fine line between selfishness and necessary secrecy drawn? In this age of population growth and limited natural resources, unspoiled places are a precious commodity. I have a number of friends who would never dream of telling anyone – not even their own mothers – where they pick mushrooms or catch salmon. In one case, a good friend took me to his secret fishing hole, a place accessible only on foot through several steep ravine crossings and nearly two miles of dense, thorny brush. When we finally reached the river, we began hooking fish after fish right away. At the end of the day, we lugged our salmon back to the car by the same brutal route. It was so arduous and disorienting, I knew then that I would never find my way back. Years later, I discovered you can actually drive directly to the spot from the other side, but on the day he brought me, that fact must have slipped my friend's mind. I completely understand.

On the other hand, in countless instances I have benefited from the generosity of others. In fact, it's humbling to count the number of times throughout my life when someone has risked sharing coveted information with me. But I like to think I earned that information through a building of relationships or some reciprocal benefit I could provide, and the understanding that secrets would be kept. Which brings me to this: Last year, after an oyster outing, the people we'd brought along came over for dinner with some of their friends, whom we didn't know. Upon entering our house, one of the women introduced herself and said, "We heard about that great oyster beach...where is it?"

If I were a smarter person, I probably would have had some diversionary, nonconfrontational response ready, like directions to another, well-known public beach. But I'm not, and I didn't. I stammered a bit, weighing the potential outcomes of various answers, and then just blurted, "I can't say." The woman roared with laughter at what was obviously (to her) a joke, then waited for my "real" answer. After an awkward silence of some duration, she said, "Are you serious? You're not going to tell me?" "That's right," I said, "I'm not going to tell you." She looked like I'd just punched her in the stomach. Another long, uncomfortable moment passed. Then she said, "Well then, I'm going to take back the marmalade I just gave you." To which I responded, by way of explanation, "If you had foraged those oranges from a secret place, I would never ask you where it was." By now, everyone in the room was watching and listening and, I'm pretty sure, at least in some cases, concluding I was an asshole.

But really, what else could I do? Did I have some kind of proprietary right to "our" oyster beach merely because I'd stumbled into the old man coming back to his car? Was I being selfish and paranoid? Probably. But, as our regional punk-poet laureate, the late Kurt Cobain, reminded us in his paraphrase of a Nixon-era bumper sticker: *Just because you're paranoid don't mean they're not after you.* Or your oyster spots.

In retrospect, I think the root of this conflict might be cultural differences between urban and rural life. The woman, who had recently moved from a big city, had no concept of foraging beyond going to the store and buying the oranges she needed to make jam. I'm sure the idea that I would withhold a source of something she wanted seemed ridiculously provincial to her, just as I was offended by her presumption that I would freely share. The assembled crowd's judgment fell into two categories: some rolled their eyes scornfully at my rude response, while others – mostly locals who have their own information to protect – believed I did the right thing. Thankfully, Stacy was in the latter group. Still, the quandary of where to draw the line remains. I mean, kids everywhere are taught that sharing is of the utmost importance, right? Well, maybe not my kids.

When someone asks Skyla or Weston where they pick chanterelles, for example, I'm proud to hear them reply, "In the woods."

When we arrive at the beach, the Sweeneys – Dan (known to most of us simply as "Sweeney"), Mia, and their girls, Maren and Laine – are already there, pulling on boots and crowding under the raised tailgate as they sort out rain gear. We've been fishing, hunting, and foraging with the Sweeneys for years, and Maren and Laine are like doting older sisters to both our kids. Maybe it's just a mood lift from the company of friends, but the rain seems to be letting up.

The tide is well out now, exposing a broad stretch of mud and gravel below the bluff where we've parked. Herring gulls ride the updraft, hovering in place like spindly white kites above the beach, and Skyla lets loose with a startlingly accurate gull cry. The birds reply, and Skyla answers back again. The familiar low-tide scent – briny, fertile, sulfuric – fills the air, and we clamber down to the water with hurried anticipation. Last year, after the same kind of chaotic first-trip-of-the-year preparation, we arrived to discover water lapping at the base of the bluff, covering the shellfish beds. I had somehow, in my enthusiasm to start the season, misread the tide book. Thankfully, it was just the four of us then, so my embarrassment was limited to immediate family. But a screwup like that stays with you, and I am relieved to see that today I got it right.

We'll pick oysters first. The clams are higher up the beach, accessible even on rising water, but the prime, smaller oysters lie along the low tide line and need to be collected right away. I pull on my gloves and gingerly walk across crunching masses of large oysters blanketing the beach. "Dad, where are our gloves?" Skyla asks, rifling through the bucket. Shit. I knew I would forget something. We are standing on hundreds of vertically growing oysters, their translucent purple-black, fluted edges razor sharp and pointed skyward. An ungloved fall means blood. Stacy and I hand our gloves to the kids, and they take off down the beach.

The adults spread out, searching. A majority of the oysters are either too big or stuck together in clumps, making them tough to shuck. The sheer biomass, though, is staggering. They are thriving here. Like most invasive species, these Pacific oysters, introduced from Japan in the 1920s, have taken well to conditions in their foreign home. Today, the Pacific is the dominant oyster in Puget Sound, having almost completely replaced the delicate native Olympia. Disturbing as this may be, the good news is the aliens are delicious. When we've filled our mesh bags, we gather around a large boulder – our shucking table – and get to work. New oysters grow from "seeds" attached to the shells, so, unlike commercially grown oysters, the shells of wild oysters need to be left on the beach to create the next generation. And so, the shucking begins.

An oyster "knife" is actually more like a blunt, flatheaded screwdriver (so *that's* why I stashed them in the screwdriver drawer...) made for prying rather than cutting. Holding an oyster with its flat side up, I push my knife into the back hinge, wiggle it to gain traction, and with a prying twist, separate the two shells. Then I run the blade along the top shell and under the oyster "body" to sever connective muscle. A quick tilt of the bottom shell, and the oyster slides into my container. But everyone has their own technique. Stacy pushes the blade between shells along one side and works back toward the hinge. Candace goes caveman style and bashes them open from any angle. After the first few awkward efforts, the muscle memory returns and we're all shucking efficiently. And, in my gloveless case, bloodily. Luckily for me, my hands are so cold, I can't feel any pain.

The kids are gathered off in the distance at the water's edge, turning over rocks and capturing the varied sea life they find. In their own plastic containers, they build elaborate homes for tiny shore crabs, sculpins, and rock pricklebacks. The big marine worms, with pincer jaws and hundreds of undulating legs along their sides, are left alone, but the slippery, eel-like pricklebacks are an endless source of wonder. Looking up from my work, I notice (with resigna-tion) Weston already in the muddy water over his boot tops and with his hands bare. No sign of Stacy's gloves anywhere. I stand and start to holler at him, but stop myself. He's gleefully splashing and laugh-ing with each rock the "big kids" turn over, and even from here I can see the huge smile on his mud-spattered face. I guess if we wanted him clean and dry we'd have stayed home.

The rain has quit, but by the time we have enough oysters, the breeze is coming up, out of the north now and colder. The tide is rising, too. If we want clams, we're going to have to hurry. With the long-handled cultivator, I dig into gravel up around the high tide line, moving along if there aren't any clams after the first cou-ple of digs. Glen hits pay dirt first, and the kids crowd around, sift-ing through the coarse sand for buried treasure. The clams here are native littleneck steamers, which in most areas of Puget Sound have been displaced (much like the Olympia oyster) by invasive Manila clams. They're both tasty, but people who eat a lot of clams generally proclaim the natives superior. I'm not sure I can tell the difference on the table, but it's good to know that there are still healthy pockets of the native species. We collect just enough to supplement tonight's dinner, place them in a bucket with clear seawater so they can expel their sand, and carefully backfill the holes we've dug.

It's time to head home. The kids are soaked, covered in mud and hungry. More than a few sets of small teeth are chattering. We gather at the base of the trail for a quick and futile sand remov-al shakedown and equipment inventory. "Where's Weston?" Stacy asks. I look up, scanning the beach, and there he is, waist deep in the cold water, facing away from us and heading out. The tide has come in, so he's not very far away, but when I yell, he doesn't seem to hear. Or he's ignoring me. I wade toward him, stopping when the water threatens my boot tops. "Hey, bud!" I call with more urgency. I can see now that he's lost in another world, peering intently into the water and shuffling ever deeper. Whatever he's chasing, it's not moving toward land. Now he's almost chest deep. I step forward and water pours into my boots, cold enough that I catch my breath. A shiver runs up my back. "Weston!" I yell as I reach him. He turns slowly and looks at me, his eyes bright and smiling. "What are you doing out here?" I ask. "I'm trying to catch that crab but he keeps scooting away," he says.

I throw him over my shoulder in a fireman's carry and we splash onto the beach and up the trail. Water sloshes from my boots and streams out of Weston's clothes down my jacket and pants. By the time we reach the car, we're both soaked. "Oh, Weston," Skyla says, shaking her head in disapproval, "oh, Weston." He's too busy laughing at his wrinkled toes to notice.

Back at the house, job one is mud and sand removal. The kids line up for the outdoor hillbilly shower – a hot-water hose bib is surely one of humankind's greatest inventions – then streak inside for dry clothes. Grown-ups kick off boots and pile them with gritty, oyster juice-soaked gloves for a mass hosing down later on. Right now, we have to get busy in the kitchen.

While Stacy builds a fire and Glen starts cracking beers for the crowd, I throw a big pot of Lundberg wild rice in chicken stock on the stove. Then I give the oysters a quick rinse and put them in a colander to drain. A sprinkle of garlic salt and cracked pepper, and we're ready to start production. First, a mix of flour and cornmeal goes into one big bowl. Next comes a bowl of eggs whisked with milk. And finally, a plate mounded with panko, the light, flaky Japanese breadcrumbs. Then it's just a matter of taking each oyster down the line in order, ending with perfectly breaded bivalves and dough-covered fingers the size of hammer handles. Meanwhile, kids are racing up and down the hallway, with Maren Sweeney playing director and big sister to the whole careening brood. Candace has the big crab pot loaded with clams, butter, garlic, white wine, and parsley. A couple of big crusty loaves from the bakery up in Port Townsend are warming in the oven. Stacy's tossing winter greens with dried cranberries, sunflower seeds, and vinaigrette. Sweeney, Glen, and Mia keep the oyster production rolling forward. Gary has a pan of mac and cheese going as an alternative for kids who might not be so enthusiastic about oysters.

If we're going to get everyone fed, I'll need to use the dreaded two-pan frying approach tonight. When the oil sizzles, I take a deep breath and start laying breaded oysters into the first pan. By the time I've filled the second pan, the first oysters are browning and ready to be turned. I have to move fast. Using long bamboo chopsticks, I get into a rhythm of lifting, turning, pulling finished oysters out and adding new ones. As each oyster reaches golden perfection, I set it on a rack and drop another one in. I sprinkle the first full rack of hot oysters with a pinch of kosher salt and slide it into the warm oven next to the bread. Reaching into the oven takes me out of my rhythm, though, and on more than one occasion, I return to my turning duty a little late. The resulting darker-than-golden oysters are advertised as "extra crispy." I'm sure a professional chef would find my task simple; for me, the frantic two-pan dance is more than a little stressful. But man, does it smell good in here.

Stacy yells "Soup's on!" and the feast begins. The crisp oysters burst with the briny flavor of the sea. Stacy has made three dipping sauces: a sharp horseradish cocktail; creamy sweet-pickle tartar; and my favorite, a mixture of soy sauce, lemon juice, and wasabi. We tear bread into chunks to absorb buttery clam broth and some use empty shells to spoon the broth directly into their mouths. A rich, citrusy amber ale from 7 Seas Brewery down in Gig Harbor quenches thirst and complements the food. We are getting down to some serious eating now.

Much to the surprise of several parents, calls of "more oysters please" ring out from the kids' table, even from the picky eaters. Nothing like a day of mud, water, and weather to build kids' appetites, especially for food they helped gather themselves. The crowd is silent, save for the sounds of eating, for the first time all day.

And then, suddenly, it's late. Our friends rush to pack up gear and load sleepy, pajama-clad kids into cars for a mad dash to catch the ferry. Where did the day go? And for that matter, what responsible parent lets small kids stay up until eleven at night? "Bedtime!" I shout to the kids while Stacy and I clear dishes and put away food. There are three oysters left on the rack, and I'm already planning the sandwich I will make with them. Skyla comes into the kitchen with her nightgown on and sleepy eyes. "I'm still hungry," she says, spotting the oysters. "Hey, I'm saving those for tomorrow," I say. "Please?" Like the old man at the oyster spot, I can't refuse her. She grabs all three, then stands at the counter eating them from her hands.

I offer what's left of the dipping sauces and she shakes her head, crunching through another bite. "No, Daddy," she says. "If you put sauce on the oysters, you can't really taste them." A purist. "Tell Chouinard I ate nine oysters tonight, okay?" she says, popping the last of them into her mouth. "Who?" I ask. "You know, your friend in Canada who always eats the crab guts and shrimp heads. He'll be real proud of me."

Later, when the kids are asleep, I step outside to clean up our gear. There's a brisk chill in the air. I can see my breath under the porch light, and water from the hose stings my hands with icy needles. Winter isn't over yet. But tomorrow we'll have three more minutes of daylight, and that's enough.

THE FOOD STARTS HERE

About the time yellow skunk cabbages open their fragrant blooms in the creek bottoms, Stacy starts getting ready for Up-potting-palooza. This will be an all-day festival of gardening, with friends, their children, yards of dirt, compost, stacks of four-inch pots, and hundreds of delicate seedlings that have been sprouting in our laundry room. It has always been Stacy's intent that her gardening efforts should produce not only food, but a sense of community. And as with most anything she puts her mind to, she's achieved both goals.

We get up early to prep for the big day. While Stacy and Weston head outside to pick leeks for soup and organize pots, Skyla and I make muffins for the crew. For expediency, we'll use my dad's "quick muffin" recipe: commercial pancake mix, corn meal (for crunchy crust), Scottish oatmeal (for chewy interior), Grape Nuts (because we have some), a pinch of salt, a little sugar, and some extra baking powder. Then we add water and Skyla starts mixing the batter while I dig through the freezer for the last of our summer blueberries and blackberries. To avoid purple-stained muffins, I give the berries a quick cold-water rinse and fold them into the batter while they're still frozen. We fill the pans, put them in the oven, and crank the heat up to activate the baking powder. Within minutes, the aroma of baking fills the house.

Outside, we help Stacy drag the picnic table into place and dump a wheelbarrow load of soil and compost on a tarp next to it. After that, I'm pretty much done. I'll help with kid control or carry something heavy from time to time, but mostly I'm going to spend the day cutting up the maple that fell in a neighbor's yard, tending berry plants, and trying to stay out of the way.

Just as I'm pulling muffins from the oven, the gardeners start to arrive. They come bearing boxes of seeds to swap, gardening tools, homemade jam, and all the news from preschool and kindergarten. Kids race into the house for muffins, then tear back outside, leaving the door swinging open.

Today's festivities might mark the physical start of our gardening season, but the process actually began months ago. Way back in the short, dark days of winter, when growing vegetables felt as unlikely as winning the lottery, we were already waiting for the signal that kicks off our gardening every year. On a raw, blustery January afternoon, it arrived by U.S. mail: the Territorial Seed Company catalog.

If there's a better entertainment value for 25 cents anywhere in the Western world, I'm not aware of it. More than a mere catalog, it's 167 pages of helpful information, mouthwatering photos, pithy writing, and, yes...seeds. Everything from Flashy Trout's Back lettuce to Super Freak pumpkins, and enough tomato varieties – 77 at last count – to conjure dreams of summer glory from the depths of winter.

These pages launched the trajectory of Stacy's year. There followed a run of late nights spent sitting by the woodstove, brow furrowed, pen cap in mouth, as she thumbed and rethumbed the pages. Then the operation moved to the kitchen table, where notes from previous years, scribbled on notebook pages and the backs of old seed envelopes, were arranged in a cluttered halo around The

Catalog. Planting maps were plotted, crumpled, redrawn. Sunlight angles and hours calculated. Page corners folded, new species and old favorites circled for consideration.

Catalog time is also the final opportunity for me to weigh in with observations from the previous year. I say observations because, as I mentioned earlier, I am for the most part a mere observer of our family's vegetable production. But as a consumer of the results, I feel entitled to offer some input.

"I think we had too many tomatoes last year," I said, recalling the slowly ripening green orbs that covered windowsills, bookcases and every other horizontal surface in our home from the first frost until well after Thanksgiving.

"So you're not going to eat any more of the spaghetti sauce we put up?"

"Oh...right. I think we need more broccoli..."

"We still have broccoli in the freezer, and nobody's eating it anymore."

"Okay, well, then...carry on."

It wasn't just Stacy, either. The kids were in on it too, like some big secret that Dad just couldn't comprehend. One February night, I asked Skyla what the best part of her day had been. "Planting seeds," she said. "You wouldn't understand, Dad."

Though my parents are both skilled gardeners – part of the original organic hippie wave of the 1970s – I did not inherit even the palest of green thumbs. And I seem to demonstrate my ignorance at every opportunity. Last winter, as she crunched through a Honeycrisp apple from the supermarket, Skyla asked if we could grow a tree from its seeds. "Nah, those are sterile hybrids...they won't hatch," I said. "And it's not the right season for planting anyway." Today, half a dozen Honeycrisp apple saplings grow in pots on the back deck where she planted them.

The seeds, then, of both this morning's gathering and my minimal participation were sown long ago. But I don't mind feeling a little left out. There's plenty of other work to do.

While Stacy and the kids take care of our vegetables, I'm responsible for the fruit. And the warming days mean I can no longer ignore my duties. Last summer, our strawberry beds were so crowded that the plants hardly produced any berries. So I decide to gamble and go for a radical, late thinning, pulling out nearly three quarters of the crowns and cutting off all the remaining foliage. When I'm done, I have a pretty good idea of what the moon's surface looks like up close. They're either going to be a whole lot better or a whole lot worse this year, but they won't be the same.

For the blueberries, I simply turn the surface dirt with a four-tined cultivator, sprinkle in some organic rhododendron food, then cover it with a couple inches of compost and water it all in. Winter took a heavy toll on the plants, and I'm doubtful about their prospects. Lots of branch tips that should be budding out are withered and gray. And there's a distinct lack of the larger, scaly buds that indicate flowers. I prune away what I can and leave some of the withered tips in place, hoping for a miraculous comeback. Is there a soil issue? Did I let them fruit too heavily last summer? Are they not getting enough sunlight?

As a backup, we bought two new blueberries – a Chandler and a Bluecrop – for the kids to grow in pots on the deck. Weston named one Cream of the Crop, and Skyla named the other Fuchsia. When there's a lull in the up-potting, the kids come over to where I'm working and we fill two big pots with compost, potting soil, and a little rhody food. Then we pull Cream of the Crop and Fuchsia from their black plastic nursery pots and examine the mass of tightly twisted roots, trying to fluff them out a little without tearing any away. Weston helps me tip the big watering can, and Skyla lies on her stomach to tell us when water runs out of the bottom. "These are your plants," I say. "If you take good care of them, and we're lucky, we might get a few berries this summer." Stacy calls this my standard Mr. Pessimism mode or "raining on the parade." I call it expectation management. "Dad," Weston says, "we're gonna have a *lot* of berries."

Our raspberries look good. The Tulameens, which bear fruit once a year on two-year-old canes, seem to have wintered well, and small, bright green leaves are already unfurling along their bare stalks. The Summits will fruit on lower sections of canes that produced berries on the tips last year, so I cut the top couple of feet off to encourage lateral growth. At ground level, new shoots are poking up through the composted steer manure I spread in November. These shoots will be the Summits' main bearers late this summer. I'm hoping for a big berry year full of fresh ice cream, shortcakes, pancakes, and freezer bags full for next winter. But then I remember that so far, no matter how much fruit we produce, the kids eat most of it before it ever gets to the kitchen.

A flicker of movement catches my attention. A tiny olive-gray bird, delicate as a hummingbird, hops through the just-pruned canes, stopping to hang upside down and peer beneath new leaves. It flutters from stalk to stalk with a distinctive, dipping flight pattern, as if tracing the shape of waves. A ruby-crowned kinglet. My favorite bird. Some years ago, when I was steelhead fishing up on the Skykomish River, a kinglet came flaring out of the brush and landed on the tip of my fly rod. I froze, letting my line swing through the current and trail below unattended. The bird looked at me carefully, and when I resumed casting, instead of flying away in alarm, it perched on a streamside willow barely an arm's length away. It kept pace with me for over an hour, watching with bright, inquisitive eyes, as I fished my way down through the long run. Since that day, I've always thought of kinglets as friendlier and more cheerful than other wild birds. But maybe that's just cheap anthropomorphizing. In any event, I stop working and watch this one, feeling buoyed by its presence.

Back at the potting table, dirt's flying and conversation is in full swing. I can hear our friend Jenn in the kitchen, running an immersion blender through a steaming pot of potato-leek soup. There's warm Dutch-oven bread from our neighbor Rebecca waiting on the table. With most of the crew hard at work and the kids still running through the yard, I slip inside to eat in peace.

I'm just about to start in on the soup when Stacy says they need more potting soil – can I go with Candace to the feed and seed store? And while I'm there, a few more bags of organic fish compost would be good. And popsicle sticks to mark the plants. And somebody needs a pair of cotton gloves... As the designated errand boy, I put the ladle down and reach for my keys. Lunch will have to wait.

By the time we get back from the store and sit down, the kids are done eating and back to their game, a complicated form of hide-and-seek involving princesses and baby kitties. It's calm and quiet in the kitchen. Still, I feel like an intruder, completely out of the loop of conversations started at the potting table. The soup holds my full attention anyway: silky Rose Gold potatoes pureed with chicken stock and grilled leeks. I have three full bowls, soaking up the last of it with a chunk of dense, chewy sourdough. Then I'm off to the neighbor's with my saw, the gardeners are back at the potting table, and the princesses and baby kitties continue running circles around the house.

At the end of the day, when the women with dirt under their fingernails and their exhausted children leave, there will be 157 tomato plants of seven different varieties planted in four-inch pots. About half will be distributed among friends and neighbors, leaving the rest to become this summer's fresh salsa, caprese salad, sandwich toppings, spaghetti sauce, and snacks. Twenty-eight broccoli starts of three varieties will accompany meals for months. Forty-four pea plants. Thirty-two bush beans. Zucchini. Kabocha squash. Cucumbers. Acorn squash. All of which I look forward to eating. Assuming, of course, that we get enough sunshine, that slugs stay under control, that the soil chemistry is right, that we thin plants enough but not too much, that the deer don't devour everything.

I tend to subscribe to my buddy Sweeney's outlook – if you expect the worst, anything short of catastrophe comes as a pleasant surprise. When dealing with the variables of nature, this just seems like the safe point of view. I may be hopeful to the point of stupidity – frequently fishing, for example, long after there's any realistic chance of success – but I never expect anything. I am, however, the lone pessimist in the family.

Stacy, Skyla, and Weston all expect the best possible outcome for every situation. Surprisingly, they are seldom disappointed. Self-fulfilling prophecy? I don't know. If you ask me, an optimist is just someone with a lousy memory. Stacy has an uncanny ability to block from her mind almost any unpleasant experience. She doesn't remember the year blight took out our entire tomato crop days before harvest, so of course she expects every crop to be bountiful. Perhaps even more telling, minutes after giving birth to Skyla, following a harrowing 38 hours of labor, Stacy declared, "That wasn't so bad. I'm ready to have another one." To be honest, I'm thankful to be surrounded by sunny personalities. But I'm not ready to convert.

Of course, up-potting day is just the beginning of the beginning. These tender seedlings will need another month or more of careful indoor tending before they can be planted outside. Stacy will also sow carrot, radish, lettuce, chard, spinach, and more broccoli seeds directly into the ground outside in the coming months. She'll stagger her plantings to keep a steady supply of ripening vegetables available and avoid the sudden overabundance of humongous zucchini or 40 pounds of broccoli going to flower. If everything works as planned, we'll eat fresh garden vegetables for four or five months and then enjoy the canned, pickled, and frozen versions until next spring.

Last year, blessed with a long, warm summer, we didn't purchase any produce from May through October. Though I haven't performed a formal cost/benefit analysis, there's no doubt this had a

major impact on our grocery bills. And eating from the garden all summer made us feel rich in ways that have nothing to do with money.

In the evening, with a soft rain falling and the scent of blossoms
in the air, I help Stacy bring trays of seedlings into the house. They
look healthy and strong, already acclimating to their new, bigger
pots. Off to the side, there's a tray of mixed plants, completely unlike
Stacy's uniform, organized rows. On the popsicle sticks standing
in each pot, written in Skyla's distinctive six-year-old hand, I read:
"brokli," "tmato" and "carits."

The season has begun. From here on out, we wait, keep up with
the work, and watch what unfolds. Looking at these small plants, I
find myself guardedly hoping for a bountiful harvest this summer.
The rest of the family expects nothing less.

THE SIGNIFICANCE OF BIRDS

I've already buried two wedges in the gnarled old fir round, and now my ax is stuck. Only one wedge left. I give it a couple of hard shots with the sledge and stop, hands tingling and ears ringing from metal-on-metal impact. The sun is finally burning through the marine cloud layer, raising an eerie ground-level mist from the damp soil. The woods come to life with birds: towhees, chickadees, wrens, kinglets, sparrows.

In the spring of my junior year of college, my best friend almost died. It was intentional, self-inflicted, and not quite successful. But it was close. And I found myself unable to grasp how something like this could happen, as they say, out of the clear blue sky.

When he was released from the hospital, we sat on the curb outside the entrance, waiting for our ride. It was April and a resurgent sun warmed the earth. The air was sweet with blooming flowers. Small birds filled a tree across the road, chattering and hopping from branch to branch. What, I wondered, could be more benign, more hopeful than this?

"Why did you do it?" I asked.

"It's spring," he said in a distracted monotone. "The birds are singing."

"Yeah...?"

"I can't hear them anymore."

A year later, also in April, I was living overseas when his mother called. He'd finally succeeded. The service would be in three days... Could I be there?

When we carried him from the hearse to the graveyard, the late afternoon sun hurt my eyes and the lawn glowed radiant green. I could see each blade of grass in sharp relief. A flock of blackbirds swooped overhead, flaring and shifting direction in unison like a school of baitfish before settling in trees along the path. I was thankful then, and more so with every passing spring, to hear the birds and feel the season.

SPRINGERS

"Wait until the dogwoods bloom," the old-timers say. But it's not easy. Pointless as it is, you spend long winter nights poring over notes from last season, plotting and planning. You have to do *something* while you wait. Then, sometime around Valentine's Day, scattered reports begin filtering up from the Columbia River – a friend of a friend got one at Kalama, someone else saw a guy with one at Cathlamet – and before you know it, you're tying leaders and working on the boat, months before it's even worth going.

Springers do that to you. Maybe it's the opportunity to chase the first migrating salmon of the year, or time on the water with fishing buddies you haven't seen since October, or the thrill of big fish in heavy spring currents. Those are all good reasons, but for me, the real motivation is the eating. There is simply nothing – not lobster, not filet mignon, not foie gras – I'd rather eat than fresh Columbia River spring Chinook. Springers are the Kobe beef of fish, aquatic bacon, chrome-plated sticks of salmon-flavored butter... A recent nutrient analysis showed that while the better-known (and highly marketed) Copper River kings weighed in with a whopping 18 percent fat content, our Columbia fish beat them – and any other wild salmon – with a luscious 22 percent. No wonder our family prizes springers above all other foods.

Once, a close relative, who shall remain unnamed, came to visit and slept in the room that also happens to house our chest freezer. At some point during his stay, tired of the compressor keeping him awake, he unplugged the freezer, intending to reconnect it in the morning. Only he forgot. By the time I discovered what had happened, everything in the freezer – most notably our last two springer fillets of the year – was a total loss. That I could barely bring myself to speak to this person for more than a year shows just how much we cherish these fish. Or, what a jerk I am.

Columbia springers enter freshwater from the Pacific in March and April (hence the name), and many won't spawn until seven months and nearly 700 miles later, way up in the Sawtooth Mountains of Idaho. Through the entire length of their arduous migration, springers do not eat, meaning they start out larded with more fat than a feedlot hog. For the original people of the Northwest, spring Chinook arrived packed with ocean nutrients just as the long, lean winter was ending, providing the most decadent meal of the year when it was needed most. For this, springers are celebrated with the greatest reverence by Native Americans throughout the region. Though these fish are obviously less critical to our survival, we nevertheless feel similar emotions about them. Springers mean more, and taste better, than any other fish.

Even cleaning one is different. Your hands become slick with grease, as if you've been wrist deep in a can of lard. The belly walls are nearly as thick as the shoulders, and the firm, red flesh is richly marbled with layers of white fat. An inch-thick steak, salted the day before and placed on a blazing hot grill, *shioyaki* style, produces the ultimate salmon-eating experience. Or, in my opinion, the ultimate eating experience, period. The skin and outer flesh crisp in the fish's own sizzling fat, locking in moisture and creating a buttery, almost omelet-like texture on the inside. And you're free to indulge without guilt. All that tasty, dripping fat comes loaded with heart-healthy omega-3 fatty acids.

It's no wonder we start dreaming about springers way too early. Frustration builds and you have to resist the pull of the big river when you know the chances are too slim to rationalize spending the time and money. If you're lucky, you still have some left in the freezer from last season. Vacuum-sealed and frozen, a big fillet can keep for months—as long as nobody unplugs the freezer. Or maybe you have one more bag of smoked springer bellies stashed away behind the last jars of freezer jam.

Eventually, the long wait comes to an end. Maybe it's the sudden predawn chorus of tree frogs or the high, reedy whistles and scrabbling claws of tiny red Douglas squirrels chasing each other around fir trunks outside the bedroom window. Or maybe it's some subtle change in the night air or a faint scent of pollen. But one morning, before you even wake, you know spring has arrived. And that means it's time to load up the fishing gear and head south.

Sweeney's has been ready for a month, boat prepped, trailer bearings greased, fuel tanks full. I mention this to point out that I'm hardly alone in my springer obsession. If we were getting paid for time spent on springer-related phone calls and e-mails prior to our first trip of the year, we could retire by the middle of March. Technology only complicates the process. On the Internet, we look at real-time stream flows in cubic feet per second, water temperature, rainfall amounts in a dozen tributary watersheds, river turbidity, and the marine weather forecast. (All of which tell us what we could determine by a quick glance at the neighbor's dogwood, but that would be way too easy.) What Stacy calls my "pretrip dithering with Sweeney" is, to us, a kind of algorithm that determines success. Sweeney has one pipeline of information, I have another, and we have to put our heads together before making the commitment. After all, it's a four-hour drive down there and a full day or more away from family and work. But there's probably a fair amount of dithering involved as well.

Finally, everything lines up. On the drive down, once we leave the interstate and start working our way west, the beauty of the country and season takes hold. Steep, heavily forested mountains plunge to the big river's edge. Waterfalls cascade down creek beds cloaked in the electric green foliage of new growth. Brightening alder thickets seem to float like pale green clouds between dark stands of timber. It's easy to imagine how Lewis and Clark, having survived their wet, miserable winter at Fort Clatsop, must have felt when they witnessed this awakening landscape for the first time.

Or 25 years later, when David Douglas, the young Scottish botanist, arrived at Fort Clatsop to catalog the unknown flora and fauna of this newest world. Reading accounts of these early explorers leads to the inevitable – and unflattering – comparisons with our own outdoor experiences. We have become soft. We cringe at the thought of a little wind chop on the water or being caught in the rain without the latest high-tech outerwear, and find the physical toughness of our predecessors inconceivable. In Douglas's day, they paddled 30-foot canoes *up* the Columbia, against the force of unimpeded current, for hundreds of miles, portaging around the Cascades of the Columbia and Celilo Falls. Portages then meant hauling massive canoes, along with all the cargo (conveniently divided into 90-pound sacks), up and around these rocky cataracts on foot. At night, Douglas felt fortunate to take shelter beneath the dripping firs that now carry his name, grateful for the warmth of a single wool blanket that was wet more often than not. Ah, the good old days.

We modern "adventurers" don't even deserve to carry a guy like Douglas's daypack. Hell, I doubt we could lift it. On the other hand, the life expectancy of early American explorers was considerably shorter than ours, and even tough-as-nails Douglas himself didn't live to see his 36th birthday. I, for one, will happily take the tradeoff.

While we may be thankful for the advances in safety and comfort (not to mention longevity) developed in the nearly 200 years since Douglas walked these shores, there is much to mourn as well. On my desk, I have a photo of a Columbia River spring Chinook taken 100 years ago that reportedly weighed 89 pounds. Eighty-nine pounds! Today, the average springer weighs in at around 12, with a really good one going 25. We're fishing for minnows.

And comparatively, very few minnows at that. In a typical year, the Columbia now receives a total run of about 1.3 million salmon and steelhead combined. Estimates based on cannery records from the 1890s provide a historical "baseline" population of between 10 and 16 million fish. And more recently, research conducted by Bill McMillan, a biologist with the Wild Fish Conservancy, shows that salmon runs prior to the extensive beaver trapping and agriculture of the 1800s (loss of beaver dams destroyed vital habitat, and unscreened irrigation intakes killed millions of juvenile salmon) greatly exceeded the cannery-record estimates.

According to McMillan, to really see what this river was like in its full glory, you have to look back even before Douglas or Lewis and Clark ever set foot here. Then, people of the Cathlamet and other Chinookan Nation tribes lived in a land of unimaginable plenty, the great river nearly overflowing with salmon, sturgeon, smelt and waterfowl. Traditional fishing sites at Celilo Falls and the Cascades of the Columbia attracted tribes from hundreds of miles around and grew into thriving centers of culture and trade. When the first foragers sat down to a meal of fresh spring Chinook, with fern fiddleheads or horsetail shoots and camas root, they had to treasure it even more than we do. And today, their descendants must feel heartbroken over what's happened to their great river.

The precipitous decline in fish size and numbers starts with the 400-plus dams – two of which buried the traditional fishing sites at Celilo Falls and Cascades of the Columbia beneath massive lakes – built on the Columbia and its tributaries. Together, these structures form the largest hydroelectric complex in the world and generate more than 21 million kilowatts of "cheap" electricity. The cost, though, in terms of salmon, has been dear. Despite the $11.8 billion spent on salmon mitigation, the Columbia's wild salmon hang by a thread.

It's not just the dams. Agriculture, heavy industry, and commercial fishing all play a role in the sad state of Columbia salmon populations. Fish hatcheries, built by dam operators as the cornerstone of their mitigation efforts, have instead contributed to the decline. Mass releases of hatchery-produced juvenile salmon outcompete their wild cousins, while hatchery adults pollute the gene pool when allowed to reproduce in the wild. Just another example of man thinking he can somehow improve on Mother Nature, I suppose. When you consider all the catastrophic changes we've inflicted on this once magnificent watershed over the past two centuries, it's incredible that we have anything left to fish for at all. So, in spite of all the losses here, I'm thankful for days like today.

After a quick and hassle-free launching of the boat – our late start does have its advantages, since every other lunatic in the state jammed the ramp long before daybreak – we run downstream and drop anchor on a shallow flat to catch the last half of the outgoing tide. Although they have an enormous river and plenty of deep water in the shipping channels to inhabit, springers, for reasons unknown to us, prefer traveling over shallow sandbars and along the shore. Once the anchor grabs, we cast our gear into the swift current and settle in to wait. And wait. And wait.

A cold east wind pushes downstream, making the boat sway back and forth despite the large sea anchor hanging off our stern. Squalls pour down from the Columbia Gorge, white curtains of whistling wind, pounding rain, and pea-sized hailstones. Sweeney calls the horizontal precipitation "eardrum rain," because of where it hits you. Last season, our first day of springer fishing saw six inches of snow cover the boat. *Spring* is a relative term, especially here.

Hours pass. Our early optimism wanes and conversation becomes monosyllabic as we hunch down into our fleece and Gore-Tex parkas. How Douglas survived this with a single wool blanket is beyond me. The old-timer next to us is packing it in. He emerges from the jury-rigged canvas rain fly above his steering console, looks up at the sky and then at us, shaking his head. "Damn east wind," he mutters, "no good for *nothin'!*"

"Fifteen minutes," Sweeney announces, "then we have to troll." The tide is almost dead low now, with only five feet of water under the boat and barely enough current to work our lures. Soon, the incoming tide will stop the current altogether, and shortly after that, the river will reverse and run upstream, bringing an end to our fishing on anchor. I start putting away the "plunking" gear and take out the trolling rigs. When I look up, my rod is bent to the handle, with line peeling off the reel.

I leap to my feet, grab the rod, and the fish streaks away downstream, then reverses itself and runs toward the boat. I reel furiously, and when I catch up to the fish, it's about a rod length off the transom, twisting and bulldogging in the current. I pull a little harder, and it comes along, still resisting but moving toward Sweeney, who's waiting with the net. I envision sizzling springer fillets coming off the barbecue, and in that moment, the fish turns to run again and the line goes slack. My lure wiggles to the surface, empty. The air goes out of me like an untied balloon. "It's gone," I say.

"What do you mean, it's gone?" Sweeney yells. Because of the value we place on these fish, we have a longstanding agreement to share all springers taken, so my loss is not mine alone. And I committed the cardinal sin of eating a fish before it was in the boat. I reel up my slack line, thinking of weak excuses, but can't come up with any worth saying. "You were thinking about eating it, weren't you?" Sweeney isn't asking, he's accusing.

The current has died now, but the weather hasn't. We crank up the motor and I inch the boat forward into the chop while Sweeney goes up to the bow to pull the anchor. "You want to bag it?" I ask. "Hell no," Sweeney says. "You?" "Nope, we're here," I say, "might as well fish." Brave words, but there isn't a whole lot of enthusiasm behind them.

The other boats in the fleet – no doubt manned by people far smarter than us – are headed for the barn. I can see their wakes through the pummeling rain, peeling off to the left toward the marina. We alone cut right at the top of the island and, running tight to shore, make the turn into the trolling grounds. Here, the wind has a much longer unobstructed fetch, and when it collides with the now incoming tide, the water stands up in sharp, rolling whitecaps. Damn east wind, no good for nothin'.

The boat pitches and rolls, wallowing through wave fronts and surfing down the backsides. We have the whole channel – normally filled with hundreds of boats – to ourselves. We slow to trolling speed. Sweeney grimly tries to keep us on course, while I get both sets of gear in the water. We seem to be fishing, but it's hard to tell. Between the wind, chop, and fast pace required to maintain steerage, I have no idea what our baits are doing down on the bottom.

"How long have we been trolling?" Sweeney asks. I pull a soggy sleeve up and look at my watch. "About four hours." "That's funny," he says, "It only feels like eight."

Almost high tide now, and we're crawling along, crabbed out at a 45-degree angle to the wind. After a long, fishless day, I cling to a shred of hope that the turning tide might change our luck, as it sometimes has in the past. The wind seems to be falling out a little, too. When we pass the abandoned cannery on the Oregon side, I dream of 89-pound springers and the good old days. With just a little squint, the peeling red paint and broken windows disappear, and I can imagine the bustling activity salmon once brought here.

Then suddenly I have a fish on. I try to snap back to the present, but find 100 years of history and a full day of sitting motionless in the cold almost impossible to overcome. My wet, frozen fingers are too numb to grip the reel, and out of desperation, I press the palm of my hand against the handle and crank. The fish somersaults through the chop, pulling hard for the far bank. When enough adrenaline enters my bloodstream to revive my extremities, I work the fish toward the boat with exaggerated caution. When it surfaces just off the port side, Sweeney makes a long reach with the net and brings our springer aboard.

I kneel down to unhook the gleaming silver slab with shaking hands and wobbly knees. Springers do that to you, especially the first one of the year. And the difference between zero and one is greater than the difference between one and any other number. We had to scratch and claw all day, but now we have a fish in the boat, and that makes all the difference in the world.

Now I can safely think about eating it. Properly bled, cleaned, and allowed to "rest" in the fridge for a day or two, this fish will become the meal we look forward to more than any other. You always hear how good fish is "fresh out of the water," and while that may apply to some species, salmon need time for their flavor and texture to develop. If you cook a salmon fillet right after catching it, you will be disappointed when the flesh curls and contracts and even more so when you bite into its rubbery consistency.

The salt *shioyaki* technique mentioned earlier further maximizes taste and texture. Ideally, you start by scaling the fish, which is easily done with a high-pressure hose nozzle before cleaning. Once I've cut the fillets into steaks, I apply about twice as much sea salt as I would if I were eating them immediately, and put them back in the fridge. The salt draws moisture out of the fish until the salinity inside the flesh equalizes. Then osmosis takes over, sucking the moisture back in and sealing the cell walls behind it. The result, when placed on a hot barbecue, is the crisp exterior and rich, juicy interior we crave. It's a traditional Japanese method; my grandmothers cooked salmon this way, as did my parents, and now me. I imagine one day Skyla and Weston will, too.

One more thing: The skin. Using a technique from the great Thomas Keller's *French Laundry Cookbook*, I take the blade of a knife and squeegee any excess water out of the skin just before cooking. Now the heat won't have to remove moisture, but will instead crisp the skin in its own fat. The first bite of Columbia springer *shioyaki* – hot off the grill with skin attached – is nothing short of perfection.

There's still daylight left, and the wind is dropping. At least it's not whistling through our lines anymore. I put the fish on ice (which hardly seems necessary, it's so cold out) and prop the cooler up on one end to tilt the fish's head down. Then I run a sharp knife inside the gill plates to cut the main arteries and allow the fish to bleed out. When blood left in the meat oxidizes, it produces an unpleasant "fishy" taste, so this step is important. Given the weather and impending dusk, we don't have time to admire this fish any further. We need to get back to fishing.

The difference between zero and one may be the greatest, but with one fish in the box, greed sets in. I hurry to get our gear back in the water. One is great. But two would be much better.

The one fish, though, has lightened our mood. Or maybe the weather really is improving? Either way, we are no longer cold or grim or tight-lipped. We laugh about the earlier part of the day as if it had happened to someone else.

Just as we cross back into the series of shallow, midchannel troughs where we got our springer, Sweeney's rod folds over and the clicker on his reel buzzes. He sets the hook, and when I see he's tight to the fish, I put the motor in neutral and let us drift. The fish comes to the boat quickly, then dives under it, and Sweeney has to scramble to get the rod tip in the water and work his way to the other side to clear the chine. The fish shatters the surface and darts away on a long run. My heart pounds in my ears. After long, tense moments of twisting back and forth just out of reach, the fish tires, and when it tips on its side, I put it in the net. We are stoked. Various celebratory gestures, embarrassing when performed by anyone over the age of 10 and not on an NBA roster, come into play.

The day has gone from brutal to decent to outstanding in less than an hour. The wind has come to a full stop and there isn't another boat in sight – something we've never experienced in this famously crowded fishery. The surface of the big river flows in a smooth stream of metallic light. A brilliant double rainbow forms against the darkening sky over the Washington side. Sweeney pauses from washing down the floorboards and says, "Where's the unicorn?"

Downstream, an eagle suddenly dives toward the water, flaring at the last moment before impact. Then, instead of swooping upward with its catch, it disappears beneath the surface, pulled under by some invisible force. In a great commotion of flailing wings and flying water, it thrashes back to the surface, clearly engaged in a frantic battle. This is better than the Nature Channel. The eagle has somehow latched onto a springer.

"Looks like he bit off more than he can chew," Sweeney says. We wonder if the bird will hold on until it drowns, and debate the rural legend that says eagles cannot release their grip, once engaged. If that were true, how would they ever let go of tree branches? But if it's a myth, why doesn't this eagle open his talons now?

Gradually, the answer becomes clear. The eagle is slowly – almost imperceptibly amidst all the chaos – dragging its prize toward shore. But the salmon isn't going quietly. It takes half an hour of incredible effort, but at last, the eagle lands its springer on a sandbar. Exhausted, the wily bird shakes out its feathers and rests beside the flopping prize. But only for a moment. Surrounded by a flurry of diving gulls trying to poach a meal, the eagle digs into the fish's succulent flesh. Validation! Sweeney and I aren't the only anglers willing to do almost anything for a meal of fresh Columbia River spring Chinook.

On the long drive home, drained by the weather and our 23-hour day, we're already planning another trip next week. Springers do that to you.

CONVERSATION WITH A SIX-YEAR-OLD

Me: (*from a cabin above the lake*) SKY-LA! DINNER TIME!

Skyla: (*no answer*)

Me: (*going down the staircase to the lake*) SKYLA?

Skyla: (*no answer*)

Me: (*reaching the dock*) Skyla, what are you doing down here by yourself? All the other families are up at the cabin eating dinner. Skyla?

Skyla: (*no answer*)

Me: Catching anything?

Skyla: Oh, hi, Daddy. Not yet, but look at all the fish.

Me: Oh, yeah...looks like a bunch of baby bass.

Skyla: They're chasing the fly around but won't bite it.

Me: Hey, it's dinnertime, aren't you hungry?

Skyla: I know, but I really want to catch a fish. See, look...they won't bite.

Me: Well, the other kids are all eating. Let's head inside.

Skyla: Dad, I just want to catch a fish first.

Me: Well...I think we need a smaller fly. Let me see what I have up in the car. I'll be right back...don't lean over the water so much. And keep your life jacket on, okay?

Skyla: Yes, Daddy.

Me: Okay, let's try this little hare's ear nymph. There. Try that.

Skyla: Look, here they come...YAAAAY! Fish on!

Me: Nice work! (*high fives*) All right, now, let's go get some dinner.

Skyla: Can we keep him?

Me: Nah, I think three inches is a little too small to eat. Let's let him go.

Skyla: Okay...bye-bye, Bassy. (*splash*)

Me: Now, how about that dinner? It's almost dark anyway.

Skyla: Dad...they're really biting now. Can't we please stay longer? I just want to catch one more...

Me: (*trying to look stern*) Well...okay. But just one more.

FIREWOOD I: INVENTORY

Madrona, Douglas fir, bitter cherry, bigleaf maple, hemlock, alder...these are the objects of my obsession, in descending order of appeal. It's no coincidence that the order reflects the BTUs produced by each type of wood. A cord of madrona produces more heat than a cord of fir, which produces more than cherry, and so on. Unfortunately, my list also happens to be in reverse order of availability. Madrona trees almost never fall, and when they do, every wood poacher on the Island races to claim them. Alders, on the other hand, tip over at the first breath of wind and tend to lie there until someone looks at his meager woodpile and desperation sets in.

Of course, each species has its own individual benefits and drawbacks: madrona, with its beautiful, sinuous form, can be tough to split and stack. When green, it splits more easily but can take a couple of years to dry. The dense, heavy wood takes a toll on your back and, if you load too much, your car springs. But boy, does it burn hot. *Throw too much madrona on the fire and you'll melt your stove*, the old-timers say. Douglas fir grows straight and tall, splits easily, and stacks beautifully. Dripping pitch can make it messy to work with, but the fresh Christmas-tree scent makes up for it. You just have to stay away from the base sections, which have a fibrous grain almost impossible to split by hand. Bitter cherry takes a long time to dry, and you have to slice the leathery bark with a knife so it'll split. Maple comes apart clean and burns well, if a little fast. Hemlock carries so much water that it's brutal to haul when green, and it produces very little heat when dry. I hate hemlock. Alder, well, not much to say about alder, other than there's a lot of it around.

Cedar stands alone for its unique properties. The oils and resins that make it our weather-resistant building material of choice – Nature's own pressure-treated lumber – also make cedar ideal for kindling. Small pieces light easily and produce the heat needed to get other wood going. And it's a dream to split. The ax slides through cedar in long vertical planes, cleaving thin, even sections of wood straight as milled lumber. You don't need a lot; all the snapping, popping, and projectile sparks keep us from using it as our main fuel. But scoring a few cedar rounds makes fire building easier all winter.

Since we generally only burn windfall or standing deadwood, we don't have a lot of say about where and when trees become available to us. Which means proximity to a road, steepness of terrain, and the density of surrounding vegetation all make a difference when assessing the desirability of a given tree. And then there's the number of side branches (knots make logs harder to split), how long the tree has been dead (green wood is heavy to haul; rotten wood is worthless for burning), and size (too big and I can't carry the rounds by myself, too small and it's a waste of time) to consider.

It has been pointed out on more than one occasion that I might be a little obsessed. You've heard about men undressing women with their eyes? I undress trees. I can't even look at someone's ornamental bonsai without mentally cutting, splitting, and stacking it.

The neighbors know I'm always looking for firewood, so when a tree falls, our phone rings. And I have to be careful about the details before agreeing to anything. Last year, for example, a neighbor called, anxious to get a recently fallen tree out of her yard. "What kind is it?" I asked. "I don't know...fir?" she said. Hmmm... "How big?" "Medium." Whatever that means. "Can I get to it easily?" "Yeah, it's in the middle of the yard." At this point, Stacy, having overheard my side of the conversation, held up a note that said *DON'T BE AN ASS*. I told the neighbor I'd take it.

I should have asked more questions. Or gone over there in person and looked at it first, but that always leads to awkward situations if I decline the offer. I've found that looking a gift tree in the mouth does little to promote neighborly feelings. When I got there with my saw, I discovered it was in the middle of the yard all right, their *back*yard. Did I mention these particular neighbors live on the edge of a ravine? The tree was about 75 yards down a 30-degree slope. And it wasn't a fir. Or medium-size, for that matter. It was a humongous green hemlock. As noted above, nothing's heavier than green hemlock. I ended up spending two long, backbreaking days cutting and hauling that sucker out of there. When it was finally dry enough to burn, it went up like balsa wood.

Another time, my friend Steve, who lives up the road and knows a thing or two about firewood, told me he had a perfect fir come down on his property. He was laid up with an injured hand, the result of a freak home-brewing accident (don't ask), so he offered it to me. I accepted sight unseen. What I didn't realize – and Steve conveniently failed to mention – was that it had fallen into a hellish patch of tangled, thorny blackberry brambles. Cutting it up was like running a chain saw in a barbed-wire factory. There was a consolation prize, though. While I was thrashing around in the briar patch, I found a huge standing-dead madrona, which Steve generously let me have. It ended up being my best tree of the year.

My preoccupation with firewood may be, as some have suggested, a symptom of obsessive-compulsive tendencies, but there is at least a little reason behind it. When we bought this house, it came with an old slab-steel Western woodstove that burned through enormous quantities of wood while producing the heat equivalent of a Bic lighter. Even a small fire resulted in vast clouds of noxious smoke pouring from the chimney. We could hardly bring ourselves to use it. After several years of outrageous heating bills, we finally stepped up and bought a new, highly efficient, Canadian-made Osburn stove. It's cold in Canada, and Canadians know how to build stoves. Its secondary burn chamber squeezes every BTU from each log and incinerates most of the pollutants in the process, producing less than 1½ grams of emissions per hour (the current EPA limit is 7½ grams). If we burn good, dry wood, you can't see even a trace of smoke leaving the chimney.

Fallen or dead trees are about as close to a sustainable, carbon-neutral heat source as we can find. A recent study by researchers at Queens University in Ontario found that modern, clean-burning woodstoves essentially produce the same amount of carbon that would be released by a naturally decaying log. We're accelerating the process, but nowhere near the level that occurs with the liberation of carbon trapped in fossil fuels. In contrast, burning propane produces 15 times more CO_2 than burning wood. If coal-fired generation plants contribute to your power supply (I was surprised to find that even here, in the hydro-happy Pacific Northwest, 36 percent of our family's electricity still comes from coal), a woodstove makes even more sense. Sure, we burn some gas cutting and hauling logs, but considering the BTUs provided by a single tree, it's a minimal footprint.

Our stove's combination of radiant and convective heat warms the entire house, allowing us to keep the inefficient electric furnace (basically a giant toaster in the crawlspace) off, for the most part. The first winter we used the Osburn as our primary heat source, we knocked 60 percent off our monthly power bill. Sixty percent! Even in the land of "cheap" electricity, this adds up fast, and our new stove paid for itself in less than two years.

The math only works if you get the wood for free, though. A cord of firewood around here goes for $150 (green alder) to $350 (dry madrona) a cord, and if you're buying it, running the giant toaster starts looking like a bargain. So, for us, it comes down to a constant search for wood and countless hours spent cutting, hauling, splitting, and stacking. Note that when I say "free," I mean that no money is exchanged, not that there isn't any cost. I pay plenty in smashed fingers, creaky joints, and the occasional back blowout.

My full-time wood obsession starts around the end of winter salmon season most years. On a routine trip out to the woodshed, I suddenly notice the dwindling stack and a certain panicky feeling sets in. Next thing I know, I'm sharpening saws and apologizing to the neighbors for not getting back to them about that hemlock that fell last November.

In our wet climate, it takes almost a full year, sometimes two, for green wood to dry. And dry is paramount: Burning sappy or even rain-wet cordwood negates all the efficiency and cleanliness of the modern stove. Even worse, it clogs chimneys with creosote, which can lead to dangerous chimney fires. Wood we plan to burn next winter needs to be split and stacked for drying by April at the latest. When I'm really on it, I have next year's wood done in February, with everything after that set aside for the following year.

The last (and only) time our beloved Seahawks made the Superbowl, I had spent the winter months so wrapped up in salmon fishing that I'd completely neglected my firewood duties. We were clearly going to be short the next winter. Wasting three daylight hours every Sunday glued to the television while our team marched through the playoffs hadn't helped any, either. We had a party planned for the big game, but a fierce windstorm Saturday night blew out power all over the Island, and the game went on without us. My buddy Glen and I spent a blustery Superbowl Sunday cutting up a giant old fir that had fallen across the neighbor's driveway. We were bummed about missing the game until we discovered that the monstrous tree had spent its whole life growing in the shade, giving it growth rings packed so tightly, it would burn like coal. I was saved from my supply predicament, and the Seahawks lost the game anyway. A year later, we were still burning that old fir long into spring.

Now it's raining again and Skyla, Weston, and I are out back stacking the last of next year's wood. A week ago, they were hunting Easter eggs around the unfinished woodpile; we're a little behind schedule. But a hot summer will make up for lost drying time, and we'll remember to burn this wood last, giving it almost a year. "Here it is, Daddy," Skyla says, handing me a medium-size chunk of fir, "the last piece of wood." "No," Weston says, "I got...this...madrona." It's too heavy for him to carry, so he's dragging the log toward me by one end. I take it from him, put it on top of the stack, and we're done.

I step back and look at a little more than six cords of wood, neatly stacked in a crisscross pattern for better airflow. A year's worth of work. Now it just has to sit there and let the weather do its job. The fir we got this year looks good for the most part, tight and dense enough to burn through long winter nights. There are a couple of nice madronas in there, too, which we'll save for serious cold snaps. The big old maple that fell in the woods behind our house is beautiful – clean and almost dry already. Too much hemlock, but what are you going to do? That pissant alder was a waste of time, but it'll burn. Do we have enough? I doubt it. But I say that every year.

OFF THE DEEP END

The robins, tiring of their winter worm diet, abandon the soggy lawn to feast on unripe salmonberries, though the hard, green fruit is so sour you can hardly touch it to your tongue. Five of my strongest new raspberry canes have fallen to some mysterious insect growing within their finger-thick stalks. The schizophrenic weather swings wildly, blessing us with warm summer sun one day, then roaring about in a fury of cold wind and rain the next.

In other words, it's May.

And that means spot prawns, although there's no natural cause for the season to take place this month. The shrimp are always there, roaming around the deep waters of the Sound. But our growing population and appetite for these succulent crustaceans has forced us into an increasingly restrictive fishery. Not long ago, people dropped pots whenever they had a taste for shrimp and the energy to pull them up from 250 feet of water. Then, to protect spot prawns from overharvest, the season was reduced to spring. And then a single month. And now, we're down to four days in May, between the hours of 9:00 a.m. and 1:00 p.m.

This creates a compressed frenzy of activity in waterfront communities throughout the area. Hood Canal, the epicenter of the spot prawn harvest, gets particularly crazy. Local sporting goods stores stack their aisles with specific, obscure brands of cat food – Puss 'n Boots mackerel reigns supreme – for bait. True fanatics mix up their own top-secret shrimp baits, the fouler-smelling the better, with recipes involving fish emulsion fertilizer, canned tuna, rotten salmon guts, herring oil, and other ingredients that I could be killed for revealing. On opening morning, outrageous lines form at boat ramps well before daylight, with enthusiastic shrimpers jockeying for launch position. All this to drop and pull shrimp pots – heavily weighted, wire mesh traps – up from 200 to 300 feet deep.

If spot prawns didn't taste so good, nobody would go through all this. Averaging six to eight inches long and occasionally even bigger, spot prawns are an oxymoron come to life: *jumbo shrimp*. And they're not just big. A spot prawn's delicate, sweet flavor and firm texture make other shrimp – tiger prawns, white gulf shrimp, bay shrimp – seem coarse in comparison.

This year, we have an opportunity to avoid most of the hassle and enjoy all the rewards. Another salmon-fishing buddy, David Smart, already has his boat on the Canal, secret bait mixed, pots rigged. Better yet, he has invited us to come along. All I have to do is show up with the kids on a certain beach at a certain time and wait to be picked up. Maybe this spot prawn business isn't so bad after all.

Smarty, as he's called by nearly everyone, including his mother, just happens to be the world's youngest old salt. He's been plying the waters of Puget Sound on a daily basis since his parents turned him loose in a miniature Whaler when he was 10 years old. Now just 26, he possesses the kind of deep, intuitive understanding of the Sound you might expect from someone three times his age. The mysteries of tide, weather, and season – so unfathomable to most of us – make perfect sense to Smarty. He'll limit the boat with king salmon at Skiff Point one evening, and the next morning, when the rest of the fleet converges there (and finds little success), he'll be 20 miles away, limiting out again at Point No Point. It happens all the time.

If you ask how he knew to make the move, his thought process is so instinctive that he can't articulate a clear answer. "It just seemed right," is about all he can manage.

Smarty drives a boat the way most people drive their cars – with the unconscious ease of something done every day for a lifetime. On the water, he'll run the boat, watch the fish finder, rig gear, catch bait, fight and net fish, all without missing a word of conversation on his cell phone. I've seen him find a football-sized crab pot buoy amid acres of heavy chop on the open Sound. In the dark. This kind of competence, though, comes with its own set of hazards. As a mutual friend says, "Smarty does things so well and so easily, he gets impatient with everyone else."

Like any good old salt, Smarty does not suffer fools gladly. And yet beneath his sometimes crusty demeanor lies a thoughtful, generous spirit. He goes out of his way to be kind to Skyla and Weston, and they both look forward to time aboard his boat. And he does share his accumulated knowledge freely with at least one fool: me. It's humbling to admit that someone young enough to be my offspring is, in fact, my mentor, but there you have it. A lot of what I know about the Sound comes from Smarty.

After four days of brilliant sunshine and calm wind, the morning of the shrimp opener dawns to a stiff southwest breeze and charcoal clouds stretching from horizon to horizon. It will be 25 degrees colder than it was yesterday. The weather service calls for rain, *heavy at times*. While the kids eat breakfast, I dig through the winter clothes bin I thought we'd put away for the year and come up with a heavy parka and ski pants for Skyla and a shelled, insulated jumpsuit for Weston. I wonder if their life vests will fit over it all.

We drive to the appointed beach, pushing our way down an overgrown dirt road with salmonberry canes scraping both sides of the car, and park where we can see the water. I keep the windshield wipers going and wait until a boat peels off from the distant fleet and starts toward us. Smarty runs full bore through the whitecaps, twin geysers of spray blowing over the bow, until he's nearly on the sand. There's no time to waste.

Everyone aboard – Smarty's mom, Helene; his girlfriend, Sammy; our buddy Neal; and his six-year-old son (and Skyla's classmate), Alex – is already soaking wet. I pack the kids into life vests on top of rain gear on top of snow suits and we waddle down to meet them. The crowd looks a little grim until Weston calls out his greeting. For some reason, he has taken to pronouncing the letter "s" in combination with other consonants as an "f": *smoke* becomes *foke*, *spider* is *fider*, and so on. "Hi David *Farty!*" he shouts. The mood lifts.

We pile in and hammer our way back out to the shrimp grounds, slamming into each wave with a spine-crunching jolt. Hood Canal is not, as the name might imply, a man-made waterway, but rather a 65-mile fjord carved by glaciers more than 15,000 years ago. When the great Cordilleran ice sheet made its final retreat, seawater poured into the steep-walled canyon, connecting it to the main body of Puget Sound. Underwater, the vertical topography makes an ideal spot prawn habitat; topside, it works like a wind funnel, gathering a brisk southwest breeze and accelerating it into the gale we're dealing with now. With apologies to Stanley Kubrick, on Hood Canal, the wind doesn't blow, it sucks.

At the first pot buoy, the real fun begins. Smarty idles up to it and Neal and I begin the two-man haul. I reach down, grab the rope with two hands and pull as far as I can, at which point, Neal reaches down and pulls. Then me. Then Neal. Five minutes into it, my arms and back burn with strain. I can feel my hands losing their grip. Smarty looks at the sonar and says "Only 150 feet to go...keep it moving, boys." And, because he's 26 years old, "Come on, let's see some of that Old Man strength."

After an eternity of cramping forearms and muttered expletives, we have the pot at the surface. An anxious crew peers over the side to see what we've caught. Smarty takes pity on his exhausted deckhands and reaches over to bring the heavy pot aboard. Forty-seven luminous orange prawns, each with a pair of glowing red eyes and long, whip-like antennae, flip around the mesh enclosure like alien bugs. Huddled in the corner, a small octopus explores its new situation with suction-cupped tentacles and a knowing stare.

Helene opens the pot lid and, with Sammy keeping count, starts grabbing shrimp and dropping them into a bucket. The count is important; limits are strictly enforced at 80 prawns per person, which is how I know we have forty-seven. The kids gather around the pot on their knees, fascinated by the creatures inside. Neal holds up the octopus and Skyla allows it to wrap a single tentacle around her finger. "Dad," she says, after it's dropped overboard to parachute into the depths, "I think we should have brought it home." "Why?" I ask, adding, "It wouldn't live long out of the water, anyway." "No," she says, "I mean to eat. They're good, aren't they?"

Smarty rebaits the pot with one hand while steering with the other, tosses it overboard, and we're already motoring toward the next buoy. The heavily loaded boat heaves through the chop, showering us with salt spray. In these conditions, it won't be easy making two more sets before the deadline.

As we approach the next buoy, Weston walks unsteadily on the heaving deck, gripping the rail with both hands, until he can reach out and tug on Smarty's rain jacket. It's taken him awhile, but he's finally mustered the courage to ask. "David *Farty*?" he yells over the wind and motor, "May you please...can I drive with the steering wheel?" He's been eyeing it all morning, enthralled by the big stainless steel wheel, which our tiller-steer skiff lacks. "We're a little busy now, buddy," Smarty says. "How about after we have all the pots in the boat?" Weston nods his head and shuffles back to the bow.

To his credit, Weston exhibits great patience. He only asks, "Is it my turn to drive?" 84 times over the next three hours. During that time, we've pulled and reset the pots twice more, collected 594 spot prawns, and reached total exhaustion. My hands curl into claws with barely enough strength to coil the lines. When the last pot comes aboard, at 12:59 pm, there is a collective sigh of relief, and we idle in closer to shore, trying to find some protection from the wind.

Spot prawns need to be cleaned and iced immediately or their flesh breaks down and softens, so everyone gets to work. Skyla and Alex grab the big shrimp out of buckets by their antennas and hand them to grown-ups, who twist the heads off and drop the tails into plastic bags. Someone – okay, me – produces soy sauce and a tube of wasabi for a quick lunch of sweet, raw shrimp tails. Weston stands off to the side, staring at the coveted steering wheel, trying to gauge whether it's time to ask again. "Weston," I say, "why don't you help the other kids grab some shrimp out of the buckets?" He looks at the big prawns flapping their tails and rocketing around in the buckets. "No," he says. "They're too feisty."

Finally, all the shrimp are cleaned, packed eighty to a bag, and put on ice. "Did somebody say they wanted to drive?" Smarty asks. Weston leaps from his perch and runs to the console, shouting, "Me! Me! It was me!" He reaches up to grab the bottom of the steering wheel and, puffed up with pride, stares ahead into the rain with fierce determination. Smarty keeps one hand surreptitiously on the wheel and eases the throttle forward as the boat putters up and over waves.

Five minutes later, Weston is still gripping the wheel, still standing up, still smiling, but now with his chin on his chest and eyes closed, rainwater streaming down his face. He's sound asleep. Helene scoops him up and he curls into her lap without waking.

Sammy has to pee. "David," she says, "I need to go to shore right now." Smarty looks at the steep shoreline and wind-driven waves breaking white over rocks. "There's no way. We'll wreck the boat," he says. A short, sharp discussion follows, and after much encouragement, Sammy accepts that her only option is to crouch in the motor well and hang out over the transom. The rest of us promise to face forward and not look back, offering what privacy is available on a small, open boat full of people. She's not happy, but, pushed by the urgency of her situation, she hesitantly steps to the stern.

Smarty idles the boat along, fighting to keep it pointed into the wind. A large cabin cruiser steams past on the starboard side, throwing a heavy wake. Smarty tries to turn into the wave to avoid swamping, but the wind pushes our bow back. He hits the throttle and we jump forward, turning just in time.

The boat rises up and over the first wake, hits a second, and then a third. Long seconds pass, and I glance back to check on Sammy. She's gone. My eyes follow our prop wash and about fifty yards back I see her bobbing silently among the whitecaps. In dreamy slow motion, I yell something and Smarty hammers the throttle down, spins the wheel, and banks hard back toward Sammy. Everyone is yelling now, scrambling around for the best position to bring her aboard. Sammy says nothing. She looks at us calmly, then reaches up when we come alongside. Neal and I grab her arm and the shoulders of her raincoat and – maybe it's the drag of her water-filled clothing, or our weakened state from pulling pots – we can't pull her over the gunwale. I feel her jacket slipping through my cramped fingers, and for the first time, a flash of panic comes into her eyes. Her legs are under the boat now, sliding back toward the prop. In a blur of more yelling and chaos, all I can do is try to hold on.

Smarty slams it into neutral, grabs Sammy's sleeve, and the three of us haul her over the side and into the bottom of the boat. Water pours out of her rain gear, flooding the deck. And still, Sammy says nothing. It must be shock from the icy water – she's safe from drowning, but her teeth chatter and her shivers look more like convulsions. Hypothermia is a very real possibility. We wrap her in towels and Smarty heads for the ramp at maximum speed, flying off wave tops, vaulting into the wind. Alex and Skyla hold on through the pounding ride, clearly shaken, and I find myself shocked, too, at the speed with which things happen. Weston, on the other hand, has not even stirred from his deep and happy sleep.

With a full low tide, the near-shore water is too shallow to beach the boat. Smarty coasts in as close as he can, then shuts the motor off, jumps out into knee-deep water, and with Sammy draped over his shoulder, scrambles up to the car. I do the same with a still-sleeping Weston and lay him down on wet sand in the lee of a driftwood cedar log.

By the time we've finished transferring shrimp pots, buoys, lines, and ice chests up to the cars and hauled the boat out, Sammy is warm and dry, quietly sitting in the car with heat blasting and Skyla and Alex chattering in her ear. She's going to be fine. Mad, perhaps, but fine. I walk back down the beach to get Weston and find him exactly where I left him, his eye sockets now filled with rainwater, small puddles with eyelashes poking through the surface. He snores softly and smiles in his sleep, dreaming of the Great Steering Wheel.

We're nearly home before Weston wakes up, and we spend the last few miles talking about dinner. Skyla says she wants the shrimp "fried real crispy," the way she had them at a restaurant in Poulsbo. Weston and I are leaning toward boiled with some Old Bay and sea salt thrown into the water. And we remember Stacy mentioned a stir-fry, something with fresh ginger, garlic, and a little black-bean sauce.

The unanimous choice turns out to be not choosing at all. Instead, we spend the rest of the afternoon in the kitchen, cooking up a spot prawn feast. Stacy cuts tender spring spinach leaves from the raised beds, dips them in boiling water and presses them into bite-sized piles. Then she pours a mix of soy sauce, mirin (Japanese sweet cooking wine), and toasted sesame seeds over the top. The kids help me prep, season, and chop all the other ingredients, then stand back and watch with amusement as I try to maintain control over the range. Finally, we sit down to a lavish meal of "shrimp three ways."

After dinner, Weston builds an elaborate diorama with his plastic dinosaurs, growling and laughing to himself, but Skyla seems a little reserved. I'm concerned she might be upset about what happened to Sammy, but I don't know how to talk to her about it. Or if I even should. "Are you worried about Sammy?" I ask. "No," Skyla says. "I know she's okay, we talked to her in the car when she was warming up." "Oh," I say, "then why are you so quiet tonight?"

"I was just wishing we'd brought that octopus home," she says. "You know, to eat."

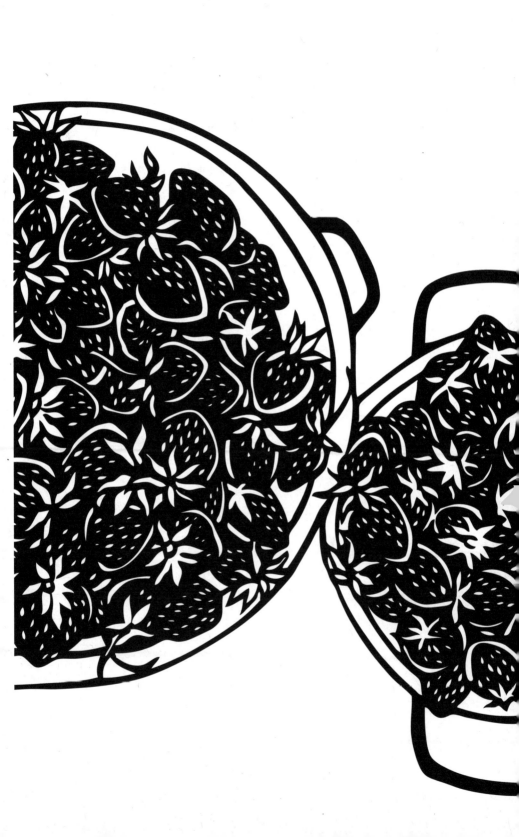

SUMMER

DIGGING DEEP

Bob Dawson is 83 years old. His wife, Joanne, is 85 and recovering from a stroke she suffered – and miraculously survived – on vacation in Mexico last winter. For the time being, she's confined to a wheelchair. The Dawsons are among the last of the Old Islanders here, country people who built their small, neat house overlooking Port Madison from salvaged lumber Bob dragged to Agate Point by boat nearly 60 years ago.

"Why don't you grab a handful of skinny sticks and your kids and come over here in about an hour," Bob says on the phone.

"What?" I say, looking for context.

"Just get the sticks and the kids and come over. Oh, and wear boots." Dial tone.

Bob grew up in the Manastash, a remote, mountainous region of central Washington, where his father scratched out a living trapping coyotes and running a mink farm. As a teenager, Bob drove the old road to Seattle and back twice a week, hauling truckloads of fish scraps to feed the minks. If he started in the middle of the night, he could make it home just in time for school, which his father required. The farm boy's work habits stuck with him long after he left home, graduated from the University of Washington, and settled here on the Island. For 40 years he worked as a schoolteacher while running a successful contracting business on the side. Generations of Islanders were educated in his classroom and raised in houses he built.

Joanne is no stranger to hard work, either. When the infamous Columbus Day storm of 1962 blasted through the Northwest with 100-mile-per-hour winds, Bob was away deer hunting. Joanne simply took their four small children down into the basement and stayed there for a week without heat, power, or running water. When she finally got through to Bob (on a neighbor's phone) and explained what had happened, he told her he'd come home immediately. She asked how the hunting was. He said pretty good, and she told him to stay there and keep hunting – they could use the meat. She's known around the Island for her years as a nurse at the local clinic, but even more for her steely resolve and quick wit.

Together, Bob and Joanne raised their family on whatever they could catch, shoot, grow, and forage. They've been jigging salmon, digging clams, picking mushrooms, hunting deer and grouse, growing vegetables, and cutting firewood for as long as anyone can remember. How they ever found time to do it all with four kids and multiple jobs is beyond my grasp. Were there more hours in the day back then?

Most of the time I can barely keep up with half the number of kids the Dawsons had and maybe a third of a "real" job. I once happened to overhear another parent ask Skyla what her daddy did "for a living." "Well," Skyla replied, "he mostly hangs around the house and goes fishing a lot." I was about to interject with a vigorous defense of my character when it occurred to me that her answer wasn't so far off base.

I do fish a lot. And, as a freelance writer, I work from home. Which leaves plenty of time to fish, cut wood, look for mushrooms, and, as a result of that freedom, worry about money. It's a tradeoff. I usually end up working in the middle of the night and trying to juggle everything else by day. Stacy designs commercial light fixtures, which allows her to work from home as well, only she does it with a lot more grace and far less complaining. I like to think that what we give up in security, we gain back through our ability to take advantage of opportunities as they arise. So, when Bob says get some sticks and come over, it's easy to put off work until after dark. I know we'll learn something and enjoy the company doing whatever he has in mind. The kids and I walk up the road, grab a handful of twigs, and head for the Dawsons' place.

Bob's in his woodshop when we arrive, putting the finishing touches on a beautiful set of cabinets he's building from trees he cut and milled himself. He shakes sawdust from his old flannel shirt and opens his brick smokehouse to hand out warm chunks of smoked salmon. "Well, then," he says to Skyla and Weston, "I guess it's time to get to work. Are you ready to get muddy?" Both kids nod.

"Why don't you go inside and say hello to Joanne while I put my boots on," he says. We open the front door and I call out to Joanne. No answer. The TV blares loudly from the other room – the Mariners are playing a day game – but still no answer. We find her asleep in her wheelchair next to a side table covered with prescription bottles. This is hardly the sharp-as-a-tack Joanne we've come to know. I motion to the kids to be quiet, and we walk softly through the house and out the back door.

Bob is waiting at the top of the stairs leading to the beach. He's got a shovel in one hand and a folding beach chair in the other. He hobbles noticeably and leans on the handrail going down the stairs, favoring the artificial knee he had "installed" a year ago. But he makes no mention of it, and neither do we. "Did I tell you I bought an airplane?" he asks with a grin. We all shake our heads. "Yeah, a Lear jet...a real dandy, too." *Pause.* "Well, I had to give it back," he says, laughing his big hearty laugh, "but with what it cost to medevac Joanne home from Mexico, they should have let me keep the plane."

It's a brilliant day. Bluebird sky, warm sun, no wind. And the tide is about as low as it will get all year, exposing a huge expanse of muddy, cobbled beach where normally there is only water. As we walk, head-high jets of water squirt out from around our feet as butter and horseneck clams respond to the disturbance. The kids stomp around and shout with delight at each new geyser. "Bob," Skyla says, "we're digging clams, right?" "Nope," he says, "we're going duck hunting." Skyla looks at him with a quizzical expression, and Bob waits a moment before delivering the punch line. "Geoduck hunting, that is," he says.

Geoducks are the largest burrowing clams in the world. They range from Puget Sound up through the Strait of Georgia and into northern British Columbia, but many scientists believe they live in greatest concentration right here around our island. The geoduck's flavorful, uniquely textured flesh makes it a prized – and extremely valuable – commodity in the Pacific Northwest, and even more so in Asia. In the native Lushootseed language, the name means "dig deep," which pretty much sums up what's required if you wish to eat one.

Unless, of course, you're a commercial geoduck harvester. Then you simply blast them out of the mud with high-pressure hoses. In recent years, the clam's growing popularity in Asia has sent prices soaring, and the state of Washington makes a healthy profit auctioning geoduck rights to commercial fishermen. At the same time, tribes around the Sound are exercising treaty rights to join in the profitable harvest. And like any highly valued industry, the geoduck fishery has spawned an underground network of poaching and black market sales. Fortunately, the commercial harvest doesn't have a direct impact on recreational diggers like us; professional divers take geoducks from deep submerged beds using their hydraulic hoses to strafe the bottom well beyond our digging areas. But this process, much like the placer mining it imitates, doesn't produce treasure without cost.

Off Agate Point, where Bob lives, the depths just offshore were once covered with eel grass and geoducks, which made ideal habitat for Dungeness crabs. We crabbed here for years, until the commercial geoduckers moved in and blew the bottom apart with their hoses. It only took two months to wipe out the area. A single dive boat, with high-pressure pumps and an air compressor that sounded like Darth Vader breathing on deck, hauled out cargo loads of geoducks, while uprooted vegetation floated to the surface. Our first crabbing attempt after they left yielded three small rock crabs and zero Dungeness. In a dozen subsequent pot drops there over the past three summers, we have not found a single legal-size Dungeness crab. Who knows how long the area will take to recover, if it ever does.

Once the Agate Point beds were harvested, the commercial divers moved east to work off the mouth of Hidden Cove, another former crab hot spot, and down the east side of the Island. It's hard to understand. Our governor and state legislators constantly tell voters "Puget Sound restoration is our number one priority," and yet significant resource extraction continues. Whether it's industrial salmon farms, waterfront development, gravel mining, or the commercial geoduck harvest, our public resource is constantly under attack for the benefit of a few private individuals. For now, though, the intertidal geoducks appear to be safe from large-scale destruction.

Today, under ideal conditions, they are showing their shockingly large necks above the mud in great numbers. Bob explains how to identify our target species by feeling the tops of their siphons. Soft and smooth means geoduck. Crusty and hard means the less desirable horse clams. With the labor ahead, we don't want to waste time and energy digging up horse clams. "Geoducks show well on a falling tide," Bob explains, "so we'll find and mark them with sticks now. Then you'll have more time to dig 'em up." So that's what the sticks are for. We walk down the beach, the kids poking at siphons and shouting either "gooey!" or "horse!"

The density of sea life exposed by the tide is astounding. Fist-size moon snails graze on algae; shore crabs scuttle about in small puddles; a single, enormous purple starfish clings to a boulder, sur-rounded by sea-foam green anemones; the mud in every direction is pocked with thousands of clam holes and shrimp burrows. The kids leap and run from creature to creature, splashing through the water and calling out, "Dad! Dad! Come look at *this!*"

When we've placed a dozen marker sticks, Bob unfolds the beach chair, hands me the shovel, and sits down. "Skilled labor's done," he says, "Now I'm going to rest and watch you guys dig some clams for us."

The shovel hits a rock one inch down next to the first stick. I move a little to the side, step on the back of the shovel and hit anoth-er rock. This goes on until I finally wiggle the blade between rocks, lean on the handle and remove a shallow divot of gravel and mud. "You're going to have to move a little faster than that if you want any clams before the tide comes in," Bob calls out from the peanut gallery. After 20 minutes, I'm soaked in sweat, covered with mud, and with my arm shoulder-deep in the hole, I can feel the geoduck's rough shell. This puts my face at mud level as I reach and strain to dislodge the massive clam.

There's nothing quite like the pungent, sulfur-salt aroma of tidal mud ripening in the sun. Especially when your face is nearly buried in it. A billion creatures, large and small, are living, dying, decaying beneath me. Using my fingers now to excavate around the clam, I eventually break the suction holding it in place and pull the enor-mous bivalve from its lie. A geoduck's neck is so long that even fully retracted, it cannot fit inside the shell. They look, in a word, phallic. And huge. Let's just say geoducks aren't the most attractive things on the planet, unless maybe you're a female horse.

But we're stoked to have this one. At about three pounds, it's an average geoduck and more than enough for a meal. Skyla says, "That's a BIG clam, Dad!" Then she and Weston get into a brief squab-ble over who gets to carry it. They settle on hauling it together, proudly presenting it to Bob, who leans forward in his chair and says, "Now that's what I call a clam!"

Turns out, twelve markers was a bit ambitious. By the time the tide comes in, we've barely managed to dig out four clams, including a monstrous 6½-pounder. Bob says it's the biggest one he's seen in years. The kids and I look at each other and laugh – every inch of our bodies is covered in black mud and sand from our efforts. Bob holds the giant clam by its neck with two hands, extending his arms at waist level, and I snap a quick photo of our trophy. He folds his chair and we make our way back up the stairs to the house.

While Bob's in the kitchen bringing a big pot of water to boil and making grilled cheese sandwiches, Skyla, Weston, and I hose ourselves off and change into dry clothes. The sulfuric mud-flat odor that permeates our hands – it won't wash away entirely for a week – doesn't stop us from inhaling our sandwiches. Joanne is awake now, nibbling at her grilled cheese and quietly staring out the window. She whispers something and I lean in closer to hear what she's saying. "Did you get any geoducks?" she asks. The kids drag the bucket over to her, tipping it so she can see our catch. She smiles with approval. And I wonder if she'll make it through this, if she'll ever be the same old Joanne again.

Lunch break is over; it's time to get back to work. We dunk the geoducks in boiling water just long enough to pop the shells open and loosen the thick, wrinkly skin that covers their necks. After a quick dip in ice water to keep the meat from cooking, the shells slide off easily and the neck skin rolls away like an old tube sock. We cut the digestive organs away from the meat with scissors, leaving two distinctly different edible parts: the solid, muscular neck and a large strip of soft, tender body meat.

For Asian chefs, it's the neck that makes the geoduck such a cherished delicacy. Too tough for cooking, when sliced thinly across the grain, a raw geoduck neck's crunchy texture and extraordinary sweetness make it one of the most sought-after sushi toppings in the world. We'll take one neck whole to slice and eat with soy, ginger and wasabi on rice. For the others, Bob sets up his ancient meat grinder and the kids take turns on the crank to make finely minced meat for chowder. I will also make geoduck dip by briefly simmering the ground necks, letting them cool, and mixing in cream cheese, seasoned salt, and green onions.

The incredibly tender body, a solid C-shaped half pound of melt-in-your-mouth clam flesh, is probably why people here go through the trouble of digging up geoducks. Once cooked, the body has a fresh ocean flavor – not unlike abalone – without any of the chewy texture usually associated with clams. I like to roll thick strips in flour, give them a quick dip in buttermilk, then another flour coating, and drop them into hot oil. For a more sophisticated meal, we'll slice the body into bite-size chunks and stir-fry them with sesame oil, soy, chili paste, and whatever fresh vegetables we have on hand. You really can't go wrong either way.

A month later, in the heat of a high-summer afternoon, we are at a big garden party celebrating Stacy's parents' 40th wedding anniversary. Tables have been set up around the lawn and the air is filled with music, conversation, and the sounds of food being served. A murmur goes through the crowd, and I look up to see Bob wheeling Joanne into the yard. She's had her hair done and she's smiling. People gather around, crouching to talk to Joanne, everyone happy to see her out.

As the bright sun fades into evening, Stacy, Skyla, Weston, and I sit with the Dawsons, listening to old Island stories interrupted by a stream of well-wishers stopping to say hello. Joanne is still smiling, but she's tired now, and Bob says they have to go soon. I remember the photo I brought, of Bob holding our trophy geoduck, and run out to the car to get it.

When I return, there are even more people surrounding Bob and Joanne. I edge through the crowd and hand the picture to Joanne, who holds it at arm's length, adjusts her glasses, and squints over the top of them. She glances at Bob and all their friends gathered around. "Bob," she says, pausing for effect and turning the photo so everyone can see it, "you look just like one of those *internet porno stars!*"

The old Joanne is back.

GIVE AND TAKE

In a couple of weeks, I will be crabbed out. Which is to say, I will have eaten so much crab in such a short time, my taste for it will evaporate. And I don't mean I'm just going to get a little tired of crab – I mean I will barely be able to stand the thought of it. But that's a future almost impossible to see now, blinded as I am by a murderous craving for the sweet, savory taste of Dungeness. Every year I tell myself to take it easy, make it last, and every year it's the same: I don't listen. I eat too much. I get crabbed out.

It's been more than six months since winter crab season closed, and our collective family anticipation is running high. Not just because we're hungry for crab, but because opening day of crab season marks the beginning of our summer on the water. Later this month, just as garden production comes into full swing, the chaos of king salmon season will engulf us. After that, big, hooknosed silver, or coho, salmon will arrive in our local waters from the open ocean. By the time the silvers disappear into their spawning streams, leaves will be falling and we'll be thinking about winter. It all starts now.

But first, the boat needs a little work. In the months ahead, it will be in near-constant use, leaving little time for maintenance or repairs beyond the nightly washings. A breakdown in July or August would be unthinkable. Time to get shipshape, as they say.

After dinner, I wheel the mighty *Lyla-Kai* (Skyla's early pronunciation of her name combined with Weston's middle name) out from under the covered carport into golden evening light. The fact that our boat might be the finest thing we own probably says more about the state of our other belongings than the vessel itself, but still, she's a beauty. With 16 feet of gently curved aluminum tapering to a sharp, upswept bow, she's little more than a car-topper compared to the hulking glass cabin cruisers that populate the Sound. Going small and light does have its benefits, though. I can launch from shallow beach ramps, tow the trailer without a monster truck, and fish all day on a couple of gallons of gas. And the fact is, we simply couldn't afford anything bigger.

We just have to watch the weather *closely*. If the weather service calls for 15- to 25-knot winds, it can be rough, and we usually think about staying on shore. Depending, of course, on how good the fishing has been. Should the forecast underestimate conditions, things get ugly fast, particularly if the wind blows against a strong tide. But most weather heavy enough to keep us off the water would make fishing from a bigger boat pretty uncomfortable anyway. That may sound like a cheap rationalization from the owner of a small boat, but it's also true.

It's not as if the *Lyla-Kai* isn't seaworthy. She was built just across the water in Snohomish with a wave-cutting, 12-degree V-bottom, plenty of beam, and a stainless steel bow rail to keep the kids from going overboard. There's enough foam under the floorboards to keep us afloat should we ever swamp the boat—a feature I hope we never have to test. At one time, there was also a fancy console with steering wheel and windshield, but I took it out to make more space for kids and crab pots. On the stern, a quiet, fuel-efficient, and – most importantly – rock-solid-reliable tiller-steer Honda outboard powers the whole enterprise.

And then there's the paint job. When we bought the *Lyla-Kai*, she was barely used, but the seller reported a "minor paint issue." Which, of course, in my lust for the boat, I ignored. The small blister on the starboard rear quarter tripled in size the first time we put the boat in the water; by the end of our first season, it had turned into shreds of loose paint dangling over bare aluminum. Beautiful. We were going to have to repaint our nearly new boat.

As I considered everything from doing nothing (easy) to painting it myself (hard, and unlikely to be an improvement), my buddy Neal, a local salmon guru who has connections throughout the fishing world, suggested I call his friend, Steve Maris. Steve owns an auto body shop and, as a serious angler, has become something of an expert aluminum-boat painter. Most of the custom-painted aluminum boats around here – including a river dory sporting wild flames down the side – come out of his shop. Since I couldn't afford "custom" anything and was leery of a West Coast Choppers look for our humble little skiff, I called him for some tips on doing it myself. His advice? Look at some paint catalogs, choose a color, and bring the boat to his shop next weekend. We'd worry about cost later. Then the guy spent three days laying down the kind of paint job you'd expect on a $100,000 German luxury sedan, for someone he'd never even met before. In return, he asked only that I pay for the paint and help his friend Kate with some story editing. I'm still overwhelmed by Steve's generosity every time I look at the boat.

While the *Lyla-Kai's* BMW Monaco Blue Metallic paint (Skyla picked the color) sparkles in the late sun, Weston helps me repack the trailer bearings with fresh grease, install a new water separator, and charge the battery. Skyla drags crab pots almost as big as she is, along with the heavy, 150-foot coils of leaded pot lines, out of the shed. One of the metal bait cages has rusted through and some connector clips are missing, but otherwise everything looks good. While I repair the pots, a brief memory of being a kid getting ready to go fishing with my own dad flickers through my thoughts. There must be something about helping with family activities that's especially satisfying for kids. Or maybe it's just the promise of adventure these preparations hold. Of course, Skyla and Weston have their moments of bickering and complaint, but I've found that such moments are rare when we're doing something outside. Watching them now, I'm thankful they seem to enjoy our work together as much as I do.

Weston climbs onto a step-stool and Skyla hands him our red and white crab buoys to stack in the bow. I lift the heavy pots over the gunwale and tie them down. The bucket of frozen salmon heads goes in the car to thaw, safe from the prying claws of raccoons. Tomorrow is the day.

With each passing summer night, the kids' bedtimes slip later and later. Tonight we let them slide even further. No one can afford to squander a minute of our precious 17-hour days, especially a warm, dry one after all the rain we've had this spring. There's still time before dark to wander through the yard and inspect our garden yet again, watching for even the tiniest signs of progress.

The early raspberries – Summits – are getting close, the fruit just starting to turn pink on canes I pruned back in March. But the cool, wet spring slowed things down. Worse, it's causing the wild salmonberry crop to fail, and hungry birds have turned to our raspberries, cherries, and blueberries to fill their stomachs. I tried "bird proof" netting and they crawled right under it. Flashing Mylar strips did nothing to discourage the feeding frenzy. Finally, I bought a plastic hawk statue marketed to suckers like me as a surefire bird deterrent. I realized it was futile the morning I watched a robin sitting on the faux hawk's head, calmly munching green raspberries. Like it or not, we are going to have to share.

June-bearing strawberries are safe inside their chicken-wire cages, but faring little better. My scorched-earth pruning technique from the spring hasn't done them any favors. They just didn't have enough time to fully leaf out before fruiting, and now, unable to gather sunlight, the stubby plants are producing small, anemic-looking berries.

Stacy's cool-weather vegetables – broccoli, cauliflower, spinach, chard – are flourishing. No danger of bolting from heat this year. Instead, they have grown thick and stocky, their leaves dark with densely packed nutrients. At dinner each night, these every-day, ordinary vegetables, simply steamed or sautéed, burst with flavor and sweetness far beyond their common reputation. They are the lone satisfaction in an otherwise gray start to the gardening season, and consolation for the sad state of our heat-loving tomatoes, peppers, and eggplant. Looking at another thin, pale tomato plant, Stacy says, "If we can just get another sixty days as nice as today, we might still be all right." She doesn't sound very confident, though.

It's pushing ten o'clock when we go inside. The kids are still wound up, too excited to fall asleep easily. An hour after we tuck them in, multiple drinks of water and trips to the bathroom are required. Later, I experience the same restlessness. It starts with calculations of tide and wind, my brain whirling with crabbing strategies, and gradually devolves into counting the hours of sleep I can still get if I fall asleep *right now*.

The accelerating bongo riff of Weston's bare feet pounding down the hallway wakes me from the deep sleep I finally fell into about five minutes ago. Bright sunlight fills the room. "Dad, Dad," Weston calls out as he charges around the corner, launching himself for a full body slam, "Wake up! It's time to go crabbing!"

While I hook up the trailer, Weston stands in the driveway, craning his neck to watch a flock of crows polishing off the last of our unripe cherries. Last year, when early spring sunshine produced a bumper crop of wild salmonberries, the birds had little need for cherries, leaving us with more plump, sweet fruit than we could deal with. That's not going to be a problem this year.

On the far side of the nearest cherry tree, above the squawking crows, I catch a glimpse of tropical color, a bright flash among the dark green of mature foliage. "Weston," I say, "look up there." I take his hand and we stalk slowly around the base of the tree, looking up through the dense canopy. The crows pay us no attention. "There," Weston whispers. A brilliant bird, a little smaller than a robin, with a fluorescent yellow breast and crimson face, perches on a twig. Compared to the subdued colors of our forest and the birds that live in it, this one looks thrillingly out of place. A rare visitor from some steamy equatorial jungle? Escapee from a neighbor's birdcage?

"What is it, Dad?" It's disappointing to have to tell him that I have no idea. Since Weston first started talking, attaching names to things has held particular importance for him. He'll walk down our road reciting plant names – *salal, black huckleberry, red huckleberry, bracken fern, sword fern, cedar* – and there isn't a dinosaur in any of the books we have that he can't name. I have to remember to look it up later so I can tell him what this bird is called. I want to know, too. It's important.

We put the boat in the water at a small private ramp just up the road from our house. This ramp, owned by the community surrounding it (of which we are not members), has been a blessing for our family, providing quick, easy access to the Sound. Because it's significantly closer to the fishing and crabbing grounds than the public ramp, we avoid the long, pounding boat rides that can be hard on kids. For years, we've used this ramp by the generous permission of friends who live there. *Of course*, they said, *feel free.*

When we first moved to the Island, one of my earliest and happiest discoveries was a longstanding tradition of generosity from people who live on the water. It was almost as though waterfront homeowners felt an unspoken responsibility to share the Sound with people who lived inland. If someone were coming to visit us by boat, a friend of a friend would hear about it and loan us her dinghy and mooring buoy without question. When crab season opened one year and we were between boats, a new acquaintance volunteered the use of his skiff. Bob Dawson invites us to dig clams on his beach and tie up to his dock. Smarty says to take his boat if we don't have time to launch ours, pull his pots if we need crab, come out for spot prawns and bring the kids. *Of course*, they've all said, *feel free*.

But things are changing at the boat ramp. Despite my best attempts to be a good neighbor (filling holes in the beach made by others, picking up litter, coming and going quietly), some in the community have taken exception to our use. Recently, notes went out complaining about uninvited guests. The combination on the gate lock was changed. The last few times we've used the ramp, we've been met with suspicious stares and pointed questions. We have become unwelcome.

Our friends who live there assure us they have every right to grant us permission. Another longtime resident said she was happy to see someone taking advantage of the seldom-used ramp. We were told the complaints came only from a handful of new residents, recently arrived from a state where property rights and litigation are the primary concerns of land ownership. *Of course*, our friends insist, *feel free*. But I don't know. The thought of Skyla and Weston witnessing a confrontation – or worse, feeling unwanted somewhere – puts a damper on what should be pure fun. And it's not like I have any rights here. I hold no grudge against the property owners who wish to keep outsiders away; it is their ramp, after all. If the situation were reversed, I might feel the same way. I am sad, though, for the loss of something that has meant so much to our family, and in a larger sense, for the end of a fine Island tradition.

Today, despite my misgivings, we use the ramp. I park the car and trailer up against the bushes where it won't be in anybody's way and skulk back down to the boat with the head-down gait of a trespasser. The kids are already aboard, clipping their life jackets. I start the motor in record time and Stacy pushes us off the beach, leaping over the bow rail. Whew. We are under way, and for now, any thoughts of angry neighbors are left behind.

We run straight out of the little harbor into the open Sound. A faint north wind riffles the surface, and I wonder how much it'll blow once the land heats up. It's reassuring to know we'll be close to the ramp in case we have to get off the water quickly, but with this thought comes a pang of gloom over our access situation. I have to consciously push it from my thoughts. Bearing west, the depth finder shows an upward-sloping bottom that levels off onto a broad flat about 100 feet deep. Smarty likes to put his pots right on the edge of this underwater plateau, close to the drop-off but not on the slope, where gravity might keep the pot doors from swinging closed. I can see his buoys just ahead. We'll run a couple hundred yards past his string to give him some space and drop two pots; then, to cover our bases, we'll put our other two a half mile east, in deeper water off the sand spit.

With the season just starting, nobody knows where the crabs are yet. But we do know where they aren't: anywhere the commercial geoduck divers blasted the bottom apart with their hydraulic hoses. Since they've gradually worked their way around the north end of the Island in 60 to 70 feet of water, we have to go a lot deeper than in the past. To find the coveted Dungeness crabs (and avoid the less desirable red rock crabs), we look for a sand or mud bottom, preferably with eelgrass and as deep as we're willing to pull pots from. For me, that's generally between 80 and 120 feet deep. No matter what, it's going to take some work.

It's not just the geoduckers who make crabbing tougher these days. With 240,000 recreational crabbers in Puget Sound, plus an intensive commercial fishery, the crabs here survive under heavy pressure. With good bait, good location, and long soaks, we still sometimes fill our legal limit of five male Dungeness crabs per person, but most of these will just barely clear the 6¼-inch minimum size. Usually, our haul is something less than the full allotment – sometimes a lot less.

Several years ago, I went up to the north coast of British Columbia to explore the Inside Passage aboard an old converted trawler. My boat mates included Yvon Chouinard, Bruce Hill, Gerald Amos, and other conservationists who had worked to preserve this section of coast, the world's last untouched temperate rain forest. Our task was to obtain DNA samples from native steelhead for research, which involved – some find this amusing – the high-tech, scientific sampling method of...fly fishing. But the reason I bring this up is that for residents of densely populated areas in the Lower 48, northward travel is a kind of time machine. Go far enough, and the years recede, revealing what used to be. Way up near the Alaska border, I experienced crabbing the way it must have been in Puget Sound 100 years ago.

One day, as the old trawler chugged down yet another spectacular vertical-walled fjord, Gerald Amos, a local Haisla First Nation leader, and I took the Zodiac and motored ahead to a small cove. While Gerald puttered around the calm waters, I baited four crab rings and tossed them overboard into 15 feet of water. When I dropped the last ring, Gerald immediately took us back to the first. Ten minutes had passed. "Pull it up," he said, a smile crossing his broad face. I figured he wanted to move the ring to a better location, but when I grabbed the rope, I could barely lift it. Still not believing the bonanza I was about to witness, I thought we had hung up on the bottom. Wrong and wrong. I finally wrestled the ring to the boat and it took both of us to pull it over the side. Inside, crabs were stacked four and five deep, many of them bigger than any I'd ever seen. Although we kept only the biggest males, the four rings yielded 57 Dungeness crabs measuring between seven and nine inches across the back in less than half an hour. From water 15 feet deep. It was then that I first grasped the seismic shift that our baselines have undergone.

It was also then that I first understood what it means to be crabbed out. We ate crab three times a day for nearly a week, mostly standing on the trawler deck stuffing our faces and throwing shells overboard. The abundance proved too much for us "southerners," our senses having adjusted to more austere foraging. By the end of the trip, nobody even wanted to see another crab, let alone smell one cooking. Except for Chouinard, who continued to slurp the pungent, steaming crab innards with great pleasure, passing the meaty legs and claws to others. That trip, 1,000 miles north and maybe 100 years ago, permanently lowered my crab-out threshold.

Back in present-day Puget Sound, with baselines fully shifted, we feel fortunate to find enough crabs for a single meal. It might not be easy, but the process is simple. We bait wire traps, or "pots," with salmon heads and send them to the bottom. Once there, the heavily weighted pots – ours have three to five pounds of lead holding them in place against powerful tidal currents – attract crabs and employ various methods to trap them inside. The inexpensive, rectangular Danielson pots have a gate on each side that allows crabs to enter and then swings shut behind them. The big, octagonal McKay has two ramps that lead crabs in, where they fall to the floor of the pot and can't escape. The Ladner, a heavy, round, commercial-style pot made with handwoven stainless steel wire, uses a combination of ramps and swinging wire gates. Each has its benefits and drawbacks, but in general, the easier it is for crabs to get into a pot, the easier it is for them to get out. For short soaks, the easy-in, easy-out Danielsons tend to fish best, while the more complex pots work better left overnight.

Today, we're moving fast and trying to cover as much ground as possible. We drop the last pot and cut the motor to drift, waiting. Stacy stretches out, lying back against the bow, eyes closed, face turned up to the sun. Weston and Skyla tear through the lunch cooler, eating, chattering, asking if it's time yet. I keep looking at my watch, willing the hands to move faster. By the time Weston has plowed through his second peanut butter–and-jelly and Skyla has counted 43 jellyfish under the boat, it's been an hour since we set the first pot.

We motor back to the general vicinity of our first pots – 105 feet of water on a line between the barge buoy to the south and the red, metal-roofed house on the north shore – and start looking. There are lots of other buoys scattered across the bay. Ours, counterweighted to stand up vertically above the surface and topped with bright orange flags, should be easy to see. But they aren't. I idle slowly through the area until I spot a flag flapping from the top of our first buoy; I edge toward it. "Keep looking, you guys, we need to find our pots," I say. Stacy sees it, too, but we don't say anything to the kids. We want them to make the "discovery."

When we're almost on top of the buoy, they both start jumping up and down, pointing and shouting. "Skyla, up to the bow," I say. "Weston, get ready." Skyla reaches over the rail and grabs the flag. As the boat slides forward, she passes the buoy to Weston, who walks it back to Stacy. Stacy pulls a few arm lengths of slack from the line, unsnaps the buoy, and hands me the line. I remind the kids that we can't all be on one side of the boat, but they're too busy leaning over the gunwale, looking into the depths. I step back to balance the boat and haul from the far side.

This first pot, a quick-fishing Danielson, comes aboard with the following: one small orange starfish, three hand-size rock crabs, two smallish female Dungeness crabs, and two big males. Not bad for a fast soak, but it could have been better. Stacy hands our two keepers to Skyla, who confidently carries one in each hand and drops them into a five-gallon bucket. Weston, still a little fearful of the big crabs, gingerly releases the other creatures into the sea and watches them sink out of sight. Now the dilemma: Drop the pot again here or gamble and keep it in the boat until we see how our other pots have fared? The crew votes to roll the dice and keep it aboard.

The second pot, 50 yards to the north, contains a single, three-foot-long dog shark that somehow pushed its way through the crab door and lies curled inside the circular Ladner. Not a single crab. I open the pot lid and carefully grab the writhing shark behind its head and ahead of the tail. The kids feel its rough, sandpaper skin and examine the mysterious, glowing-green deepwater eyes. The shark splashes us with a stroke of its tail when I drop it overboard.

Our pots off the sand spit have been in the water for nearly two hours by the time we reach them, and I'm not sure if it's the longer soak, the slackening tide, or just a better spot, but combined they produce eight keepers, along with a dozen undersize and female crabs. Or it could be Stacy's mojo, since she pulled these last two. Whatever the reason, we have stumbled into an unexpected jackpot. We reset these pots and drop the others nearby.

The original plan was to find a decent concentration of crabs and leave the pots to soak overnight. But the first pot of our second round comes up with four more keepers. If the remaining three pots produce at all, we'll have more than enough. Hello, gluttony. The bucket is already overflowing, and big purple-tan crabs scuttle all over the floorboards. We stow this pot and move on to the rest. When all four are aboard, we have 18 keepers and we're all moving carefully to avoid stepping on crabs. It feels like we just hit the lottery.

We load the boat onto the trailer, escape the ramp without incident, and on the short drive home, bask in the satisfaction of a big haul. I even manage to back the trailer through the obstacle course that is our driveway – around the cedar stump, inside the big fir, between the rhododendrons – on the first shot. I believe this is what professional athletes refer to as being "in the zone."

I hook up our propane crab cooker – sold as a turkey fryer in other parts of the country – in the driveway, fill the big pot with water and add salt until it tastes just a little saltier than seawater. I can keep an eye on it while washing down the boat and trailer. I'm also watching the cherry trees for another glimpse of the bird we saw earlier, still wondering what it was and hoping for a closer look.

When the cooker lid rattles, I drop six crabs into the roiling, salty water, hit the timer on my watch, and try to pay attention to my boat-washing duties. It isn't easy. Every time the breeze shifts, a cloud of fragrant crab steam wafts toward me, and my mouth waters.

Weston runs out of the house carrying our dog-eared Sibley bird book. "Here's the Sib-i-ly, Dad," he says. "Can we look up that bird?" I knew there was something I was supposed to remember. We open the book. "Is this it?" I ask. "No...Dad-dy! That's a mallard." I flip a few more pages. "How about this?" "That's a spotted towhee." I keep turning pages, until finally, "Dad! Dad! There it is. Go back." It's as exciting for him to find the mystery bird here in a book (and attach a name to it) as it was to see it live. He's right. There it is: western tanager. Having never seen one before, I'm a little disappointed to read that it's considered "common." No exotic tropical visitor here. Weston, though, isn't bummed in the least. He says the name to himself a few times, a look of deep satisfaction on his face, then runs back into the house, shouting, "Mom! Skyla! We found the yellow bird!"

The crab cooker boils over, sending a cascade of foam down the side and a more intense blast of crab vapor into the air. I adjust the flame to simmer. We're almost there. I give up trying to wash the boat and instead stand idle, watching the proverbial pot boil. Five long minutes pass, and then, finally, it's time. I pull the scalding, brilliant red crabs from the water with barbecue tongs, rinse them off, and set them on the picnic table to cool. Six more live crabs go into the pot.

The moment I can touch the cooked crabs without getting third-degree burns, I start pulling carapaces off and scraping guts and gills into a bucket. My grandmother would have scrambled the intensely flavored, mustard-colored innards with eggs, soy sauce, and sugar, then served them over rice for a true Japanese delicacy. Chouinard would simply slurp the steaming guts directly from the shell. But not us. Even though the Sound is cleaner than it's been in decades, its legacy as an industrial waterway keeps us from partaking. We'll stick to the meat for now.

Stacy brings out a loaf of whole-wheat sourdough, a tasty, edible napkin for wiping crab juice from hands and faces. We sit at the picnic table and start cracking shells. Everyone has favorite parts: Stacy and Skyla prefer the satiny, snow-white body meat that falls from cartilage compartments at the base of each leg; Weston carefully pries small, tender morsels from the back legs; I go for the big, thumb-sized sections in the front legs and crumbly, robust chunks from the claws. Pieces of shell fly through the air, crab juice drips from our chins – *please pass another chunk of bread* – and the feeding frenzy is on.

There will be a time later, maybe tomorrow or the day after, for Stacy's crisp, savory crab cakes, an omelet or two, crab and melted cheese on toast. For now, all I want is crab in its purest form. And lots of it. Knowing crab doesn't keep well only fuels my hunger. I drop the last shells of my first crab in the bucket and, still chewing, reach for another. What was that about taking it easy? I can already see the wall coming, and yet I'm helpless to stop myself.

But wait. Bob and Joanne Dawson could probably use a few crabs, as could Marc Bale, and our next-door neighbors. I could give Steve Maris a call too. And our friends who let us use the boat ramp, they might like some. Why didn't I think of it before? *Of course*, I will say, *feel free*.

THE SIGNIFICANCE OF BIRDS II

Smart, gregarious, inquisitive, but above all else, survivors, crows adapt to any environment, from deep wilderness to inner city. They are the mischievous black streak that snatches a potato chip from the inattentive picnicker. The goofy clown unable to resist a shiny piece of broken reflector in the driveway. The fierce defender chasing an eagle many times its size away from a nest.

My mother says Grandma is a crow now. I'm not sure if I buy it, at least not in a literal sense. Yet I can't help feeling a special affection for the big black birds. And if Mom's right, Grandma is, at this moment, hovering above the mailbox, dropping clams on the pavement.

When we first moved here, we found all sorts of strange objects on the small patch of asphalt near the mailboxes: steamer clams, crab claws, walnut shells. It was a great mystery. Who was putting them there? Was it a neighborhood kid's joke? Some kind of sign?

One morning, Skyla and I heard a great commotion and cawing...and the mystery was solved. Crows had discovered they could bring objects they couldn't crack with their beaks to the road, and let gravity and pavement do the work for them.

Now, on our way to get the mail, Weston and I watch with pleasure as "Grandma" swoops and flutters, dropping her clam from increasing heights until, finally, it breaks open and she dives in for her well-earned snack.

I still can't say whether I believe Grandma's spirit actually lives on in these birds. But if seeing a crow reminds me of her, what difference does it make?

SUMMER, EVENTUALLY

The old-timers like to say that summer starts here on the fifth of July. They say it half in jest, with knowing smiles and shoulders shrugged toward a rainy June sky, but more often than not, they're right. In western Washington, parkas and tarps are as important to Independence Day celebrations as fireworks and barbecues. The wisdom of our elders, though, is easily forgotten. After two summers of consistent warmth and sun, we assumed we'd be watching fireworks in our shirtsleeves forever. We were wrong.

Of course, it's easy to dismiss old-timer weather lore. How many times can you hear "When I was your age, we had snow on the ground up to here" without rolling your eyes? *Yeah, and let me guess, you walked to school barefoot, and it was uphill both ways, right?* But, it turns out, Pacific Northwest weather really was colder and snowier "back in the day." Over the past four decades, the annual snowfall here has averaged about six inches. But between 1949 and 1969, Seattle weather records show that almost three times as much snow – 17.4 inches – fell each year. In January 1950 alone, the Island got five feet of the stuff. Maybe it really was uphill all the way to school and back in those days, too.

This year, we seem to be returning to the chilly days of yore. We've had a few stretches of seasonable weather, but for the most part, spring has stretched into what the calendar calls summer, with gray skies and frequent rain. I try to take Annie Dillard's wise words – "there's always unseasonable weather" – to heart, but this is getting ridiculous. The heat-loving vegetables are growing to Seussian proportions, cartoonishly long and leggy, reaching upward for a sun that remains obscured by clouds. Global warming? Dr. Nathan Mantua, a prominent atmospheric scientist at the University of Washington, says that one possible outcome of a warming planet would be cooler, cloudier summers in Puget Sound. So we have that going for us.

We celebrated Fourth of July bundled in fleece and blankets, crowding around a bonfire at a friend's beach house. Melted butter we'd planned to serve with a big bucket of fresh crabs solidified before we could use it. The kids stayed inside the house to escape the cold and wind, building elaborate living-room forts until the fireworks were about to start. Stacy, Skyla, and I watched the showering sparks and starburst explosions hunkered in the lee of a giant drift log. Weston – despite urgent parental requests to stay dry – splashed into the cold, dark water, throwing rocks and whacking sticks. On the drive home, Stacy and I wondered what becomes of all those shell casings and burnt chemicals raining down on the harbor. The weather hasn't helped our family mood.

There are some bright spots, though. A nesting pair of Pacific slope flycatchers has taken up residence in the awning above our back deck, entertaining us with their midair, insect-snatching maneuvers. I happily tolerate nesting materials raining down on the barbecue in exchange for the flycatchers' pest extermination services. And boy, do we need them. The wet weather has produced a bumper crop of mosquitoes, the huge, clumsy ones that first appeared in February steadily giving way to ever smaller, faster, and more fearsome biters.

"Musquetors very troublesom," wrote William Clark in 1806, when he and his men discovered that bear grease and tallow – apparently the 19th-century version of DEET – did little to deter the hordes of biting insects they encountered. This spring, inspired by the exploding mosquito population, I quoted Clark at every opportunity, carefully enunciating his distinctive misspellings. For some reason, Stacy failed to find the humor in this.

Fortunately, our flycatchers work like living bug zappers, perching on one specific tomato cage from which they launch their aerobatic sorties. The tomato cage also functions as the flycatcher outhouse, and it's no surprise their poop has killed the Stupice tomato that grew there. I'm okay with that. Not to count our tomatoes before they ripen, but that still leaves us with 72 plants, far more than we'll need if they produce at even moderate levels.

We have owls too. A mated pair we welcome, like the flycatchers, for their predatory habits. Earlier this spring, we were overrun with mice. Crossing the yard, you could see them pushing wakes through the grass ahead like scattering fish in shallow water. I trapped an unending stream of rodents from the house, the shop, and, much to Stacy's horror, her car. If there'd been any kind of market for mouse pelts, I could have opened a modern-day Hudson Bay Company and retired on the profits. But the last time I checked, mouseskin coats had yet to appear on the red carpet, so I was left with the disgusting chore of clearing traps and burying carcasses each morning.

Then the owls moved in. From the first night we heard the barred owl's distinctive, four-note call – frequently described as "who cooks for you?" but to me sounding more like "*whoo, whoo, huh-whoo?*" – echoing through our woods, my "trapline" production began to diminish. A month later, you couldn't find a single mouse anywhere on our property. Soon a new sound joined the hooting: a blood-curdling, raspy shriek, like a cat hissing into a megaphone. The new baby owl was calling out to his parents, hungry for more mice.

One morning, I came face to face with the baby owl, perched at eye level on an alder branch. Huge, almost-human eyes stared directly into mine from a disheveled bundle of gray fluff. The hair on my neck stood up and I shivered, first from the shock of meeting this enormous bird, then from the thought of its mother, gliding on muffled wings with talons extended toward my scalp. It happens. Frequently enough that the city has put up warning signs in local parks where joggers have been attacked by barred owls. On this morning, there was no winged assault, but I walked the rest of the way home awfully fast.

In a cruel irony, owls around the world are disappearing at alarming rates, victims of powerful anticoagulants used to control rodent populations. These "second generation" mouse and rat poisons were introduced in the 1970s to kill the pests with a single dose. There's a good chance you have a box or two sitting on a shelf out in the garage. The problem is that a single dose can take up to five days to work; in their weakened state, the poison-filled mice become easy prey for owls. These poisons were found in nearly 75 percent of dead owls examined in one Canadian study, and are, according to *Scientific American*, "imposing a toxic load on the environment that no one bargained for." In our attempts to control pests, we're poisoning the predators that would naturally control them, which requires us to use more poison, which...well, you get the picture. I'll take the owls.

My only complaint is their voices, booming around the yard starting at dusk and continuing off and on through the night. I love to hear their wild, spooky calls, but *in the distance*. It's a little different when they're perched on a branch 10 feet from your bedroom window. However, given the alternatives – a swarming, unchecked mass of rodentia or the lethal brew of chemicals it would take to kill them – I'll take the hooting.

You can only eat so many strawberries. It's not that we tire of them; we just can't keep up with the sudden abundance produced by even a modest patch of June-bearing strawberries. Assuming, of course, the modest patch in question hasn't been butchered by inept gardening. As previously reported, my late, radical thinning effort – exacerbated by the lousy weather – resulted in a weak early crop. Now, after months of just barely hanging on, my little plants have finally matured into complete failure.

Luckily for us, we are not relying on my gardening skills to put food on the table. Because the trees surrounding our little clearing in the woods keep growing upward, our home garden gets less sun each year. It's like living in a slow-motion sinkhole. To boost production, Stacy does a lot of her gardening at a small farm plot just up the road. It's an open, sunny hillside tilted to the west for maximum warmth, with rich, well-drained soil. The owner has generously opened up the land, free of charge, to a community of like-minded organic gardeners, and crops grow there with miraculous intensity.

Stacy's plot came with a small patch of feral strawberries left behind by the previous gardener. Unaided by helpful hands like mine, the berries are thriving. In early June, Weston came home from the farm with a single, slightly smashed strawberry he'd saved for me. "One strawberry?" I asked. "Well," he said, "there were three, but I already ate two." It was delicious, sweet, and dripping with deep red juice. Two weeks later, he was bringing home baskets full.

Now it's time for our first real food processing of the year: strawberry ice cream. We start with our standard recipe, whisking plain low-fat yogurt, half-and-half, a little sugar and a dash of vanilla in a bowl, which I put in the fridge to cool and blend. Skyla slices strawberries into another bowl, while Weston uses a potato masher to "smoosh" an equal amount into pulp. We sprinkle a little sugar on the combined berries and chill them in the freezer. After dinner, we turn on the electric ice cream machine and add the cold yogurt mixture, and when it starts to thicken, the kids take turns spooning almost-frozen strawberries into the mix. We eat two heaping bowls each and read bedtime stories with full stomachs, still thinking about the ice cream. Then I head back out to my office. I have a story deadline hanging over my head and I need to make some headway. But three hours later, I'm back in the kitchen for another spoonful. If there's a more heavenly dessert, I can't imagine what it might be.

Later in the season, we'll get more creative. We always try to beat the birds to a few handfuls of early blueberries and raspberries, which we mix with more strawberries and buttermilk for an intense, dark purple, three-berry ice cream. It's so fresh and light, we eat most of it straight from the machine, and freeze what's left in popsicle molds.

Finally, at the peak of the strawberry harvest, with bins piling up in the fridge and more coming home each day, Stacy makes freezer jam. It's a serious project, with huge pots of boiling berries, sugar, and pectin steaming away on the stove. She ladles the hot, translucent red liquid into the peanut butter, pickle, and mason jars we've saved all year, then leaves them on the counter to cool. Overnight, the pectin works its magic, setting the liquid into perfect, spreadable jam that somehow tastes more like fresh strawberries than fresh strawberries themselves.

Like many houses on the Island, ours was built on land once covered in strawberries. Marshall strawberries, to be exact. Now listed as one of the 10 most endangered food plants in the United States, the famously sweet, juicy Marshalls drove the Island's economy for years. At the peak of production, just prior to World War II, local farmers – with names like Suyematsu, Oyama, Nakao, Katayama, Koura, and Terashita – shipped nearly two million pounds of berries off the Island during the brief harvest season. In 1939, these berries became a lasting source of civic pride when they were served to King George VI and Queen Elizabeth of England as part of a feast representing the best foods of North America.

Mike Terashita, whose parents farmed the land we now live on, tells stories of the incredible industry that came to life around the Island during the harvest. His father would drive up to Vancouver and bring truckloads of First Nations tribal workers down to help with the picking. The seasonal workers lived in the many outbuildings still standing near the Terashita house, and Mike's mother cooked for the crew around the clock. There was a bustling cannery in the harbor to process the bountiful crop, and a steady stream of shipping traffic hauling canned and fresh berries to the mainland.

But the Island's strawberry industry didn't last. When the federal government forced Japanese-American farmers into relocation camps during the war, the farms suffered and the cannery was abandoned. Around the same time, the fragile Marshall plants were besieged by new diseases inadvertently brought onto the Island. Moreover, times were changing. A growing consumer preference for fresh berries doomed the Marshalls, which had a short two- to four-week harvest season and even shorter two-day shelf life. Today, all that remains of a once booming industry are the weather-beaten shacks still scattered around the Island, an annual Strawberry Festival, and the memories of those old enough to remind us that "Marshalls were the finest-tasting strawberries in the world."

Summer struggles to emerge, and our tomatoes, eggplants, and peppers struggle to survive the low temperatures. The cool-weather crops thrive. Stacy's strategic planting of broccoli, spinach, and lettuce in two-week intervals brings a constant stream of maturing produce. Zucchini and pumpkin vines sprawl along the ground, and their huge yellow flowers, although late, show promise. Inside our little greenhouse – actually more of a green lean-to made of corrugated fiberglass siding attached to the garage – three types of cucumbers snake upward on bamboo lattices. A small side bed, basking in reflected heat from the house, pumps out baskets of bush beans and arugula. It doesn't feel like farming weather, but we're eating well.

A joke Skyla made up and told to the produce manager at our local grocery store: *What's a coyote's favorite vegetable? Ar-ar-ar-AROOOOOOOOOOOOOOOOOOOOGULA!*

King salmon season won't open for a couple of weeks yet, but I want to be prepared. Actually, I've been getting ready, at least mentally, since the last season ended, almost a year ago. Now, with the first migrating summer kings on their way in from the ocean, it's time to get serious. We've been out crabbing, but those are casual, easy trips compared to what's coming.

The boat's running lights need to be fixed for predawn and post-dusk fishing, and the trailer's brake lights are shot. Just part of my ongoing battle with the corrosive effect of salt water. To get the upper hand, I'll replace all of the lights with sealed, waterproof LED units, and commit to more meticulous freshwater wash-downs. I also need to check our safety gear – flares, horn, fire extinguisher – and reorganize the boat, exchanging the crab-pot pulley and measuring gauges for rod holders, fish box, and the big salmon net.

And then comes the fun part: tackle. As with every new season, there are fresh strategies to try and theories to test. This year, I'm planning to fish faster and cover more water, which means I'll need heavier weights. I also want to catch more live herring for bait, so I have to tie up some herring jigs and double-hook mooching leaders. There's a whole drawer full of the latest, greatest fish-catching lures that I couldn't resist as I wandered through various sporting goods stores over the winter. I'm a sucker for the shiny new spoons, rubber squids, and a plug shaped just like a herring. Most will probably be duds, but you never know.

I spool fresh line on the reels, sharpen hooks, and freeze some milk jugs full of water for the fish box. This year, we're really going to get 'em.

It's July 5, and once again, the old-timers were right. Summer arrived suddenly today, as if somebody had flipped a switch, dark skies turned brilliant blue; chilly air gave way to warm, almost tropical humidity. And now, tonight, I toss and turn in bed, listening to the owls through open windows, my mind racing with thoughts of king salmon and the approaching season. I get out of bed and walk out onto the back porch. Owl calls boom back and forth through the velvety night air. A choir of frogs and crickets swells, suddenly falls silent, and swells again on some mysterious cue. To the east, the starry black sky fades to deep blue; it's going to be light soon. Summer is here.

FIREWOOD II:
PRODUCT MANAGEMENT

Blue tarps, freight pallets, five-gallon buckets: the unholy trinity of hillbilly yard art. Accumulate enough around your house and you're either the punch line to a Jeff Foxworthy joke or you're getting serious about firewood. I prefer the latter, but the truth is, we're probably a little of both. When you live out in the woods, your collection of these things just seems to grow on its own; next thing you know, you're dragging your best blue tarp off the woodpile to wrap rusting kitchen appliances in the yard. Or spreading it over the '72 Camaro up on blocks out front, and tuning up your banjo. It's a slippery slope.

But we're not all the way there yet. For now, the three icons of modern rural life function mainly in the service of our firewood production. Here's how:

First of all, it's *blue*tarp. One word, two syllables, emphasis on the first. If you want any kind of credibility whatsoever, you need to get your pronunciation right. Second, it rains like hell around here, so tarps – and plenty of 'em – are critical to properly curing the firewood that's going to keep us warm all winter. Let me backtrack a bit here. If you've stacked your firewood to allow decent air circulation, a little, or even a lot, of rain is okay early on. The process of soaking and drying helps green wood rid itself of sap. But toward the end of August, rain-wet cordwood won't dry before you need to burn it. That's when blue tarps come into play. I keep our wood stacked out in the open for as long as possible, letting the sun and wind do their work. But at the first hint of late-summer rain, out come the tarps. When the sun reappears, I pull the tarps off and the curing process continues.

When the tarps start to be on more often than off, it's time to move all the dry wood into the shed. And it's important to remember that the drying process won't continue inside, even though I've ventilated the shed walls with so many holes they look like Swiss cheese. Any residual moisture leads to mold and lousy burning. One year I left a cord of alder out in the rain uncovered and thought it had dried enough before I packed it into the back of the shed. By the time we'd burned through everything in front of it, the stack had turned into a putrid wall of fuzzy mold. There were even mushrooms sprouting from it. It was so frightening, I spent several hours researching rental hazmat suits. When this proved fruitless, I pulled a painter's mask over my face, hauled the whole pile way back into the woods, and burned my clothes when I was done. Then I went out and bought more blue tarps. You can never have enough blue tarps.

Pallets are the foundation of our entire firewood enterprise. We get ours from the local lumberyard, where every Tuesday worn and partially broken pallets are left out in the parking lot for the taking. Whenever I'm driving by and have room in the car, I stop and grab the best of the pile. Sometimes you need to replace a broken board or two, but over time, you end up with a pretty decent collection.

Any wood left in contact with the ground here soaks up moisture, even during the summer. Pallets are perfect drying racks, ready-made to keep air flowing under firewood. Our shed floor is made up of 14 pallets wedged into place and leveled with bricks, boards and whatever else was handy. Outside, the length of the shed is lined with more pallets, buried under double rows of recently split, drying wood, which will be moved inside once it has finished curing. Up by the driveway we have even more pallets, holding a slowly growing supply of rounds waiting to be split. You can never have enough pallets.

And then there are the plastic buckets. Mostly we use the round, five-gallon variety that once held paint, stain, or drywall mud. Some were left over from our house remodel, but I'm not sure where the rest came from. They just seem to appear and join the rotation. Buckets are ideal storage containers for dry kindling, with the benefit of built-in handles for easy hauling up to the house. When they're empty, I take them back to the shed, where Skyla, Weston, and I form a kindling production line. From a pile out back, we drag pieces of splintered cedar siding, which I split into long, narrow strips with the ax. Then the kids stomp these into lengths that fit our stove. Busting kindling is fun. Weston, fully outfitted in rain boots and swim goggles (my safety glasses were too big) leaps onto each cedar strip with both feet, yelling, "HI-YAAAA!" Skyla, also wearing swim goggles, works much less theatrically and at twice the rate of the Karate Kid. The buckets fill up fast, and we haul them to the house feeling good about our work.

The utility of plastic buckets, though, goes far beyond firewood storage. Maybe that explains why we have so many. One holds all my wood-cutting gear (chain-saw oil, sharpening files, plastic wedges, measuring stick, folding handsaw), another contains a full set of clamming equipment (mesh bags, lantern, extra mantles, matches, gloves), and yet another is set aside for hauling road-repair gravel. The nice clean ones, especially if they have lids, haul crab bait, crabs, dry clothes, and fishing gear in the boat. I even use one special "food grade" bucket to brine turkey breasts for smoking. The uses are endless: Got some raspberry canes waiting to be planted? Stash 'em in a bucket. Need to bleed a salmon out quickly? Cut the gills and put it head down in a bucket of water. Digging up more beets or potatoes than you can carry? Better bring a bucket. The plastic five-gallon bucket, then, is the duct tape of containers – a versatile, practical solution to most any problem. You can never have enough plastic buckets.

Before you know it, the yard ends up festooned with tarps, pallets, and buckets. And you're contemplating a step up to the hillbilly-deluxe level, which involves 55-gallon oil drums and 40-foot steel freight containers. Like I said, it's a slippery slope.

Now, a month after the summer solstice, the days are growing imperceptibly shorter. Common sense tells us that the earth should be cooling, but instead, the weather lags behind, as it always does, and we bask in the heat of high summer. Prime wood-drying time. In the weeks to come, the wood stacks will shrink a good four or five inches in height as moisture escapes and logs shrink.

Next month I'll have to start paying closer attention to weather patterns. Last year I gambled and lost trying to squeeze in a few extra days of drying time. An unexpected front moved through before I could haul the tarps out, and I spent a nervous few weeks in September hoping for Indian summer to fix my mistake. I'm not going to risk it this year.

If we can get a solid week of warm, sunny weather in early September, I'll take it. A dry north wind would make it even better. Then it's a full weekend spent moving firewood into the shed, and a surprising sense of relief when it's all safe. After that, bring on the rain.

Standing here squinting into bright July sunshine, I find these future labors almost as hard to imagine as the cold, dark winter ahead. Could night ever really fall at 4:30 in the afternoon? Will I stand in this very spot shivering in my down parka? It hardly seems possible. Across the yard, Skyla and Weston spray each other with a hose, running and sliding on wet grass. Stacy's in the garden, tying up tomato vines to support the growing weight of still-green fruit. A bumblebee buzzes past, headed for the late-blooming raspberries. I look back at our long rows of drying wood. Do we have enough? I doubt it. You can never have enough firewood.

YOU CAN'T EAT DAHLIAS

Stacy was supposed to be here an hour ago. Skyla, Weston, and I, having concluded our morning fishing, idle the boat just offshore, turning slow circles in the hot sun, waiting. The plan was for the three of us to fish while Stacy worked at the farm plot, then she would meet us at the beach to pick up the kids on her way home. Weston would get his nap, Skyla her playdate, and I could keep fishing through the afternoon tide. But she's not here.

Another half hour passes, and I can feel my impatience winding up like a spring. The good fishing tide comes and goes. Finally, her car emerges from the forested hillside. I run the boat up on the beach, feeling grumpy about wasting time and tide. Waves beat the boat up against the cobbled shore and I quickly lift the kids out and set them on dry land. When Stacy walks down to meet us, I make an exaggerated show of looking at my watch and say, "What happened? We've been waiting almost two hours." She doesn't say anything. I look at her more closely and see a pale, greenish cast showing through her sun-browned skin. Her eyes are red and watery. "I've been on the side of the road throwing up," she says, her voice shaking. "There's blight at the farm."

A week of heavy rain and warm temperatures put a layer of mold on ripening raspberries and powdery mildew on the broad leaves of zucchini and squash. We already knew there was some trouble in the garden, but figured that if seasonable weather returned, we could deal with it. But blight, that's something else altogether. Some say it lives in the soil and splashes onto plants when it rains; others believe it arrives with the rain itself. One thing everyone agrees on is that when dark blotches appear on tomato stalks, there is no hope. Four years ago, late blight hit our tomatoes just before ripening and our frantic, all-out efforts to save the fruit proved futile. Last week, when rain started falling through warm, humid air, a collective dread rose in the gardening community. A few days later, there were whispered rumors of blight. Not that anyone actually admits they have blight; it's so contagious that if you show up with a blighted stalk at the feed and seed, people flee in horror. Nobody wants the Black Death.

While the term "Black Death" may sound melodramatic when used by modern recreational gardeners, it's worth noting that our tomato blight is the same fungus that caused the Irish Potato Famine. Within a year of its appearance on Irish farms in 1844, blight had wiped out nearly half the national crop. The result was catastrophic in a country where potatoes had become the primary food source. Nearly a million people starved to death, and twice that number left the country in desperation. This little fungus brought hunger and tragedy to an entire country and changed the course of world history. More than a century and a half later, it still carries a heavy load of residual dread.

When Stacy got to the farm this morning and saw black spots on stalks that had been a healthy green yesterday, she knew it was over. The heat-loving tropical tomatoes, already weakened by our late spring and cool summer, were sitting ducks. All the months of labor and coddling were wiped out overnight. The 72 remaining plants from all those seedlings started in our laundry room back in March had to be destroyed.

She had spent long, sweaty hours digging up her cherished plants and stuffing them into a burn barrel. It was heartbreaking work. On the way to meet us, she was overcome by nausea and cold sweats so powerful she couldn't drive. Whether it was heat exhaustion, emotional distress, or a toxic effect from so much contact with the plants themselves (tomatoes, like potatoes and eggplant, are close relatives of poisonous nightshade), it was hardly the joyful day of garden work she had anticipated. After my initial greeting, belated attempts to offer comfort feel lame and insincere to both of us.

I push the boat off the rocks and watch them drive up the beach road and out of sight. Hardly the joyful afternoon of fishing I had imagined. And it's not just the blight, either. We can always buy tomatoes at the store; they won't be nearly as good, but we aren't going to starve. What I'm really upset about is me.

In my experience, you rarely catch fish when angry ("Don't fish mad!" they say), and I doubt that's going to change this afternoon. My bad juju sends out negative energy the way boats with ungrounded electrical systems pulse with fish-repellent voltage. I can't shake my mood and, predictably, I fail to find a fish in the next two spots. After a distracted pass through a third, I decide to pack it in. It's just not going to happen today.

I load the boat on the trailer and drive up through town on the way home. Passing the grocery store, a new thought occurs to me: We haven't bought produce in months. Even with today's loss, the garden has hardly been a failure. Through sheer effort, Stacy has willed a plentiful harvest from the garden in spite of all our lousy weather. We've had armloads of green, yellow, and purple string beans; long, crisp Japanese cucumbers; bunches of chard and spinach; four kinds of carrots; enough broccoli to eat five times a week; mixed salad greens of trout's back lettuce, romaine, and peppery arugula; pungent basil; more zucchini and crookneck squash than we know how to use; sweet, earthy golden and red beets.

We're up to our eyeballs in beets. Last month, Stacy and her friend Jenn drove up to a large organic seed farm in the Skagit Valley, where acres of experimental beet cultivars were about to be tilled under for compost. They returned home with five-gallon buckets full of beets stacked to the roof of Jenn's van. We ate them boiled, steamed, roasted and sautéed, barely putting a dent in the supply. Finally, Stacy brought out the canning gear, filling shelves throughout the house with sweet pickled beets, savory canned beets, beet relish... If you happen to find yourself running short of beets, give us a ring. We could use the shelf space.

A brief side note on beets: If you're going to eat them in any quantity, it's important to remember you ate them. I repeat, remember that you ate beets. I won't go into details here, but let's just say that the natural red color – often used as organic dye – does not break down in the digestive tract. If you forget, there will come a moment of utter terror, and perhaps an unnecessary trip to the doctor. Trust me on this.

The fact is, we've been eating like royalty for months. There were fresh garden stir-fries with ginger and oyster sauce, salads every night, sautéed chard in garlic and olive oil, buttery parmesan zucchini, Kabocha squash braised to the texture of roasted chestnuts. The steamed broccoli was so sweet you wondered if it was really broccoli. *Nasu dengaku* became a favorite treat, made from sliced Japanese eggplant coated with miso, sugar, and soy and broiled to caramelized, jammy perfection.

The blight has left our potatoes alone (at least so far), and the kids revel in digging through the mounds with bare hands to find them. We've used the golden German butterballs for gratins bubbling with cream, butter, and cheese. (So much for my cholesterol count.) Small, creamy reds we've boiled and cubed for potato salad. Fluffy Rio Grande russets have become hash browns, bakers, and, mixed with butter and sour cream, mashers good enough to make a main course. With more still in the ground, we'll store what we already have in a cool cabinet and enjoy our "buried treasure" all through the winter.

And really, it's not as if we won't have any tomatoes. Before she pulled the doomed plants that had yet to show blight symptoms from the ground, Stacy harvested a dozen flats of uncontaminated green fruit. These will slowly ripen in the coming months on windowsills. They will not be the glorious, sugary, vine-ripened tomatoes we hoped for, but there will be plenty. And the indoor-ripened versions, with their lower sugar content, make salsa and spaghetti sauce more to our taste anyway.

Despite Weston's attentive care and fervent wishes, his watermelons didn't pan out this year. The vines came up and grew but languished for lack of sunlight and heat. Flowers formed on the stunted plants, eventually producing three rock-hard, dark green melons about the size of golf balls. They molded away without ripening. But he's already looking forward to the "big sweet ones" he'll grow next summer.

Then there are the dahlias. When Stacy first planted them, I protested, saying we needed food, not flowers. "Why waste time and space on decoration?" I asked. Of course, she ignored me and went ahead. Looking back, I couldn't have been more wrong. Especially in what has been a cool and gray summer, these otherworldly explosions of color provide a kind of nourishment I did not foresee. I know, it sounds corny. But to wake up on a foggy morning and see radiant blooms through the bedroom window, to find them glowing from a vase on the kitchen table, to stop and watch a tiny, fluorescent-green tree frog nestled between burgundy petals...somehow lifts the spirit. It's a value that's difficult to quantify, but a value nonetheless.

There's one kind in particular, called Tequila Sunrise, with volleyball-sized flowers of astonishing design. Brilliant yellow dissolves to warm peach tones on the outer petals, gradually gaining intensity toward the deep orange center of the bloom. How could anything be more perfect? On my way through the yard, busy with this or that, I frequently pause for long moments to marvel at its beauty.

The garden has fed us in many ways this summer. Beyond the meals and flowers, there is the image of Skyla and Weston making deliveries to our neighbors, their baskets overflowing with vegetables they helped grow. There have been boxes of produce to help feed needy families. And there's the community of gardeners that has grown up around the farm plot. All of this is Stacy's doing. I resolve to tell her how important her work is to the family and how much it means to me.

When I unhook the boat and walk around the side of the house to get the hose, I see the dahlias – fuchsia, pale pink, hot orange, deep crimson, sunshine yellow. A tangle of dark green summer squash and tricolored Northern Lights chard sprawls out below. Hidden somewhere in the foliage lies the behemoth zucchini the kids are saving for the harvest fair.

Stacy slides the kitchen door open and comes outside. She's changed clothes and showered, and though her eyes look tired, her color is returning. I put my arms around her. "I'm sorry about the blight," I say. There's more, but I haven't figured out how to say it yet. She hesitates, then pulls in closer to my chest. I can feel her damp hair on my neck. "So am I," she says, "So am I." We stand there together for a long time, looking at the dahlias.

KINGS OF SUMMER

It always comes as a surprise. One day in late August, you look up from the hectic blur of summer activity and realize that things are winding down. It might be a blue-sky, 85-degree afternoon, but something in the angle of the light, or a single falling alder leaf, tells you the season is waning. Autumn is right around the corner.

Fishing for king salmon has slowed over the past week, most of the fish having moved through the Sound and into their rivers. Yesterday we fished for eight hours without a bite. The day before, one small fish all day. It's been a good season: We've eaten fresh kings several times a week, there are bins of smoked salmon in the fridge, and most important, the freezer's full.

To be honest, even though I look forward to king season all year, the end is kind of a relief. The early wakeups, the long days on the water, the late-night boat cleaning, the constant vigilance over weather and tides take a toll. I'm tired. My back hurts and my hands are wrecked from saltwater and sun. We've been rolling on at a crazed pace since the middle of July.

For our family, king salmon season is what deer season is to other rural families: an all-hands-on-deck effort to secure the year's main protein source. While I'm out on the water, Stacy shoulders the burden of managing both the garden and two energetic children. Then there's work. Every year, I try to clear the calendar for July and August, and every year, inevitably, writing projects pop up and I have to juggle deadlines with prime fishing times. I feel fortunate to have the work (the mortgage needs to be paid), but for these months, it's one more factor in the madness.

So, as the season comes to a close, there is relief, but also a touch of melancholy. The end of king season also signals the end of summer. All those warm, sunny afternoons and 10:00 p.m. dusks; the camping trips and barbecues; the bike riding and beach splashing – how did they get by us so quickly? The longest days of the year pass faster than the others.

Silver salmon should be here soon, along with blackberries to pick. With the first autumn rains, chanterelles will push up through the damp forest floor. The best weather of the year – Indian summer – is still weeks away. But a sense of urgency descends upon us with the lengthening shadows and earlier nights. Soon, it will be time for kids going back to school, soccer practice, swimming lessons. For regular bedtimes, early dinners, and catching up on work. For schedules set by forces other than wind, sun, and tide. And at the back of my mind, even though it's a long way off, I'm already preparing for winter.

But first, one last day of king fishing. Or rather, one last weekday on the water with Skyla and Weston before school starts. King season is technically still open, but we've spent most of the summer trolling, and last week, Skyla reminded me again that what she and Weston "really like is to hold the rods." So today we'll drift bait for flounders and sharks. We won't eat them, though. A century's worth of accumulated industrial pollution in the Sound makes year-round bottom dwellers less than ideal for human consumption. This will be a strictly catch-and-release affair. And while the kids are committed catch-and-eat anglers, they're still excited to hold the rods, feel the bites, and reel in the fish themselves.

Our day together also buys Stacy some uninterrupted garden time. Although blight may have taken out the tomatoes, the rest of the garden is in full swing. There are weeds to pull, beds to water, and beans, cucumbers, zucchini, beets, carrots, and squash to pick. The pressure canner, vac-sealer, and dehydrator won't be put away for a month. It's harvest time, and she's in full production mode. A day without her junior assistants will increase efficiency.

Since we're committed to a bottom-fishing expedition, there's no pressure to be on the water at first light or for a certain tide. The kids and I sleep in, eat a leisurely breakfast, putter around the yard, and put the boat in the water at the public ramp. We run south out of the harbor, then make a big, looping turn back to the north once we've cleared the shoals. The air is dead calm, the surface of the Sound a broad sheet of unrippled blue silk. With our light aluminum skiff, it's a rare day when we can go full blast. Weston shouts, "Go faster, Daddy!" I twist the throttle wide open, the bow drops, and we shoot forward like an arrow.

There's only one other boat off the point, a couple of old guys trolling for kings in a vintage Whaler. We coast in alongside to set up for our drift and get a report. "We've been pounding it since 4:30 this morning without a bite," the driver says. They continue on their troll and we lower our baits to the bottom. The flounders and dogfish are biting. Both kids stare intently at their rod tips, feeling the bites, hauling back and reeling furiously to see what's on their lines.

Weston pulls a flounder over the side, and as I'm unhooking it, Skyla says, "Dad, they have a fish on." I stand up just in time to see the old guys lifting a big slab of writhing chrome into the Whaler. King salmon. A good one. Five minutes later, they're hooked up again. I'm starting to rethink the whole flounders and dogfish thing, but the kids are enjoying themselves, so we stick with it. But now I'm watching the Whaler like an eagle.

When the old guys put a third king in the boat, Skyla says, "I think we should troll." With flounders and dogfish forgotten, we hastily rerig for salmon. "You sure you guys are okay with this?" I ask. "You won't be holding the rods anymore." Skyla looks at Weston, gets a nod, and says, "We'd rather try to catch a king salmon." I put the rods in their holders and start the motor.

But we don't catch a king salmon. An hour passes. The guys in the Whaler boat a fourth king for their limit and start packing up. As we putter by, Skyla whispers, "Ask them what they're using." I ask, and the driver answers, adding, "You just gotta put in your time. We fished seven hours before our first bite." Then they crank up their motor and roar off toward town.

Another hour passes. Weston, having announced he is ready for his nap, curls up on the floorboards and falls asleep. Skyla keeps a fierce watch on her rod tip. The sun broils all of us. "You want to go back to flounder fishing?" I ask. She shakes her head without looking away from the rod. "You want to go home?" Another head shake. "It's really hot out here," I say. "Maybe we should head in."

"Dad," she says, impatient with me. "We just have to put in our time..."

Well, okay then. Skyla helps me check the gear and we continue on. With no wind – or salmon – to deal with, and the kids content, I let my mind wander back through the season.

Opening Day – just six weeks ago – up at Port Townsend, our annual multifamily camping trip to kick things off. Anticipation ran high with the whole season stretching out ahead of us. After a long afternoon of setting up tents, stacking firewood, and organizing camp, Stacy suggested that Sweeney and I go fishing. There was a stiff breeze out of the northwest and a lousy tide, but we put the boat in the water anyway. Out on Midchannel Bank, the wind whipped around us and a vicious chop made fishing nearly impossible. The boat rocked and pounded, floundering in the waves. Minutes after I asked Sweeney if he thought we should be worried about safety (his answer: "Possibly"), the portside rod hammered down. In less than an hour we hooked five big, ocean-fresh king salmon and put four in the box for a ridiculously quick limit. When we pulled back into camp, Stacy said, "What did you forget?"

A week later, my mom came to visit. Stacy was busy in the garden, and the heat made cooking dinner indoors less than appealing. A little picnic on the water sounded perfect. The fish had yet to arrive here locally, but I figured we might as well drag some gear around while we ate. About a mile south of Kingston, where the bottom slopes up from 150 feet to less than 80, we were busy watching an osprey hunting along the shoreline when I happened to glance at the rod. It was shaking furiously and I knew right away our gear was dragging bottom. I grabbed the rod and felt solid resistance. Dammit. Hung up on a snag. Just as I threw the motor into neutral, line started peeling off the reel and...fish on! The kids took turns fighting the big king – their first ever – and my mom got to be part of the excitement. When the fish came aboard, we all hugged and danced around the boat. As they say, better to be lucky than good.

I think of the early morning trip with Smarty, when he was supposed to be at work by nine and we'd fished too long. On the way back in, he was frantic, running the boat wide open, skipping from one wave top to the next, asking for the time every three minutes. Halfway across the big open stretch south of President's Point, he said, "I just lost the steering." "What?" I yelled, thinking I must have heard wrong. He looked back at me and spun the wheel around several times to demonstrate. The boat kept going straight. And fast. But he refused to back off the throttle – this being the middle of king season, he was already on thin ice with his boss. We somehow made it across the Sound, into the harbor, and right up to the dock by dragging a five-gallon bucket on alternating sides of the boat to steer. He made it to work on time, too, but I'm pretty sure my arms are several inches longer from hanging on to that bucket handle.

And there was the long run up to Possession Bar with Scott Orness, when the incoming tide stacked schools of herring up against a big underwater ledge on the west side. The baitfish (and the salmon feeding on them) were 200 feet deep. To reach them in a ripping current, we had to put out so much line we couldn't turn the boat without fouling the prop. A rising crosswind made it even worse, and we were reduced to fishing one rod on the upwind side of the boat. When we finally hooked a fish, a seal grabbed it right away and ran for the horizon. Our only hope was to stay directly on top of the seal, forcing him to let go of the fish if he wanted to surface away from the boat. The tug-of-war lasted more than thirty minutes. Every time we thought we had him corked off, he'd shoot out to the side, come up for a quick breath and go back under. Eventually, though, we wore the seal down, and when he opened his mouth, the fish shot straight for the boat and into our net.

And just last week, when Skyla started our fishing day by saying she wanted to see porpoises "in real life." With this new priority, we spent the day fishing places out in the open Sound, where salmon had been scarce but the porpoises, both the small, dark harbor porpoises and the larger, black and white Dall's porpoises, tend to feed. It was flat calm and I thought finding them would be a cinch. But hours passed and we didn't see a single dorsal fin or plume of blowhole breath. Finally, I told her we might as well forget porpoises and just concentrate on trying to catch a fish. We ran to the back of a small bay where fish had been holding and started to troll. Skyla was distracted, scanning the surface for porpoise fins instead of watching her rod. "You can relax," I said, "they won't be way back in here. Let's just fish." Of course, minutes after I spoke, two sleek black forms materialized behind the boat, came up alongside and kept pace with us. Porpoises. Here? They splashed and swam upside down, weaving back and forth under the boat while Skyla leaned over the bow rail squealing with delight. I was about to say *this never happens,* but didn't.

"Dad," Skyla says, calling me back to the present, "there's sea-weed on both lines." Lost in my mental slideshow of summer high-lights, I've driven us right through a tide rip full of eel grass and sea cabbage. She's right: Both lines are fouled. Skyla cranks the gear up, using both hands on the reel handle, and I lean over the side pull-ing handfuls of vegetation off our gear. Weston sleeps through the whole process. The sun, directly overhead now, roasts us. I realize I've forgotten to bring sunscreen. Both kids have pink cheeks, and Weston, the fairer of the two, is flat on his back, face to the sun. Bad dadsmanship. I pull Skyla's hat down lower on her face, drape a sweatshirt over Weston's head and hope for clouds. When we're clear of the weeds, we put the gear back down and resume fishing.

Another hour passes. Weston sits up, pulls the sweatshirt off his head, and with sleepy eyes and red face climbs onto my lap to wake up. I breathe in the clean, sweaty-head, sleeping-kid smell of his hair. Funny, the things you come to appreciate. "I'm hungry," he says. "Me, too," Skyla says. So am I. "Okay," I say, "let's head in and grab a snack in town on the way home." They both shake their heads. "What else did you pack in the ice chest?" Skyla digs out the last, sad-looking salmon sandwich, partially flattened by the ice pack, and tears it into three pieces to share. It tastes wonderful.

Maybe it's my hunger, or the sandwich itself, but I can hardly look back through the season without reliving the great meals we've eaten. As John McPhee wrote of king salmon, "Their dense, rud-dy flesh – baked, smoked, or canned – is one of the supreme gifts of nature." Indeed. I think of the thick early-season male fish, the bucks, heavy with fat and perfect for salt-broiled *shioyaki*. And the females, the hens, already transferring body fat to their eggs, mak-ing them much better brined in salt and brown sugar and smoked over vine maple. Every time I cranked up the smoker this summer, the savory aroma spread through the woods, and neighbors seemed to drop by a little more often.

The deep red, translucent salmon eggs themselves are even better. I push them through quarter-inch hardware cloth to separate the individual eggs, and then rinse them quickly in saltwater. They cure in a little soy sauce, rice wine, and sea salt for about three days, and then I freeze them in small jars. I try to save these cured eggs – *ikura* – for special occasions, but usually end up eating them right away. We savor them over rice or on crackers with cream cheese, or, as Skyla and Weston prefer, simply by the spoonful. Skeptical friends, wary of eating "bait," are quickly converted upon first taste, and it's tough to build up any kind of surplus in the freezer.

I'm not sure if it's genetics or personal taste, but for our family, and Skyla in particular, there is a deep preference for the oiliest, fishiest parts of the salmon. When everyone else is eating choice center-cut fillets or steaks, she requests the collar, or *kama*, as my grandmother would call it. This cut consists of the bony plate behind a fish's gills and the front pectoral fin socket. Eating it requires the patience to dig through and disassemble the intricate bone structure to find tender, oily morsels within. I usually brine the collars with a batch of fish headed to the smoker, then throw them on the barbecue until they're crisp on the outside and dripping melted fat. Skyla likes to sit down to a big king collar hot off the grill and a steaming bowl of rice; with each bite, she closes her eyes and chews slowly, chuckling to herself with pleasure. When one of her school friends once watched her eating a collar and exclaimed, "That's gross!" Skyla replied between bites, "That's not gross...that's *kama*. It's the best." Add crisp, tart, thin-sliced garden cucumbers from the garden, marinated in rice vinegar and mirin, and sprinkled with toasted sesame seeds for contrast, and I'm right there with her.

With the lower fat content of late-run fish like the ones we've been catching the past few weeks, we favor cooking methods that either add fat or preserve moisture. If we're having a party, we'll make what Skyla calls bacon-wrapped yum-yums. I slice the salmon into boneless one-inch cubes, wrap them in bacon, and marinate them overnight in teriyaki sauce. We'll skewer these and grill them over hot charcoal until the bacon crisps and the teriyaki caramelizes, leaving the salmon medium rare. When it's just the four of us, we roast fillets in foil or parchment pouches with butter, parsley, garlic, and lemon. For a side dish, the kids dig small red potatoes from the garden and Stacy makes mashers with sour cream, butter, and chives. Then the familiar debate: Crisp, lightly-steamed bush beans or sweet, second-growth broccoli? Often we go with both.

And this brings me back to the sandwiches. I take any leftover cooked salmon and mix it with mayo, a squeeze of lemon juice, dill, and cracked pepper. Sliced wholegrain sourdough from the local bakery, buttered and sprinkled with garlic and grated Parmesan cheese, goes into the broiler. When it's crisp on one side, I take the garlic bread out and spread a thick layer of the salmon salad on top, followed by lettuce, thin slices of fresh cucumber, red onion, and tomato, and a light dusting of kosher salt. It's a sandwich I could probably eat every day for the rest of my life.

It's been a good season, full of small miracles and memorable meals. A great season, really. And all the days we've spent on the water this summer will come back to us in the fall, winter, and spring with each fillet we take from the freezer. Looking at the kids in the late afternoon light, I hope that someday they'll share summers like this with their own children.

The prospects for the future, though, are not bright in Puget Sound. Wild king salmon are in grave danger of extinction, and the hatchery runs created to replace them are not sustainable. The plan to improve on Mother Nature is backfiring because of the simple fact that hatchery salmon, raised in a perfectly controlled environment, hand fed, and protected from predators, never undergo the all-important process of natural selection. Weak genetics are passed on and amplified, and each year the fish return in fewer numbers and smaller sizes. Fifty years ago, the average Puget Sound king salmon weighed nearly 25 pounds. Today, the average weight is about 12.

And an overwhelming majority of recent scientific studies show that the very presence of hatchery fish exacts a terrible toll – through competition and "genetic pollution" – on the few remaining wild salmon.

Our family's fishing is entirely dependent on hatchery fish. We are required by law (and conscience) to release any wild fish we happen to catch, and still their numbers are low enough to warrant a federal Endangered Species Act listing. The factors causing this decline are human. We are the enemy, and I don't think we're going away anytime soon. Industry, population growth, development, resource extraction, and runoff from failed septic systems, car leakage, and lawn chemicals combine to make Puget Sound a tough place for salmon to survive these days.

Not long ago, Seattle school kids restored a local urban stream for their class project. When the work was done, they planted juvenile coho salmon and waited patiently for them to return from the sea. When the first autumn rains fell two years later, the students came back to welcome their fish home. They watched in horror as wave after wave of fish entered the stream, immediately went into convulsions, and died. Water tests later showed that a combination of lawn chemicals and toxic metals from automotive brake dust had poisoned the water.

What can we do? I really don't know. On an individual level, we can try to make as little impact as possible, and this kind of consciousness seems to be spreading. More people are growing and eating organic food, driving less, letting lawns go natural, composting their waste, saying no to consumerism as a way of life. The question is, will that be enough? Salmon are a totem to all the cultures of the Pacific Northwest, and as such, they hold special importance for most of us who live here. I hope this status can somehow help our elected officials, corporations, and individual citizens make the sacrifices necessary for long-term salmon survival. I realize, of course, that those sacrifices might include giving up the fishery that means so much to our family, but we can accept that if we know it's making a difference. I sure would miss it, though.

The uncertainty about how many more seasons we might have ahead of us makes each one all the more precious. And here at the tail end of another good one, even on a fishless day, I'm happy to be on the water, fishing for kings with my kids. The sun has dropped below the high, fir-covered ridge that rises up behind the point, and I'm relieved. The kids won't be hammered with UV anymore. It's not evening yet, but long shadows are already stretching out over the water. I can almost feel the earth starting its seasonal tilt, pulling us farther away from the sun.

"One more pass," I tell the kids, "then we have to go or we'll be late for dinner." We troll out along the deep trough that runs parallel to the beach, and head east toward a set of old, decaying pilings that mark the best water. We pass the pilings without a bite and continue out past the point, beyond where I've ever caught a fish. It's so calm, we might as well keep the gear fishing while we clean up the boat and get ready to head in. I'm dumping the last of our flounder bait over the side when Skyla yells, "Dad! Dad! Fish!" Thinking she's seen a silver jumping somewhere, I look up and scan the horizon for rings on the water. "No! No! *On the rod!*" she shouts.

The portside rod is bucking in the holder and line is streaming off the reel. I pick it up, set the hook, and feel a powerful headshake at the other end. The line rises through the water and 100 feet out a king salmon leaps into the air, shattering the glassy surface. I hand the rod to Skyla, kneeling next to her to help, and she cranks the reel handle while I hold the upper cork grip for support. I look at the other rod and realize I don't have a free hand to clear the line. "Weston!" I say, trying to sound calm, "reel up the other line. Just keep it in the holder and reel." Then, leaving the motor in gear to avoid tangles, I start the boat turning in a wide arc.

The fish makes another run and jumps, then dives for the bottom, tiring. Skyla is tired now too. "Okay, Skyla," I say, "Let's give

Weston a turn. You get the net." I hold the rod and Weston grabs the reel handle with both hands. He can barely make any progress, but slowly the fish turns and comes toward us. I want this fish for the kids so badly, my stomach churns with adrenaline. Now, the tricky part. I brace the rod with one hand, tell Weston to keep cranking no matter what, and kick the boat into neutral. Skyla has the net handle, which is half again as long as she is, balanced over the gunwale with the hoop in the water. As the boat glides to a stop, Weston and I lean back and guide the exhausted fish toward the net. When it's within reach, I let go of the rod, grab the net ahead of Skyla's hands and together we lift a gorgeous, big, bright king into the boat. Unbelievable. Skyla throws both arms into the air and shouts, "*YES!*"

After the fish is bled and iced and all the gear is sorted out, I take my salmon tag (which the state uses to calculate harvest) and sit down to record our catch. My hands are still shaking. "See, Dad," Skyla says, "We just had to put our time in. Now we're going to catch a bunch."

I reset the gear and we turn back to fish over the submerged point where we hooked our king. Normally, I'd run upcurrent at full speed and then troll back through the spot with the tide, but time is short and it seems doubtful that there would be more than a single fish here. One more quick pass. And three minutes into it, the other rod pounds down. This fish runs straight out to the side, then comes to the top thrashing before I can get the rod out of the holder, and when I come tight to it, the hook slips from its mouth. Instead of diving into the depths, the fish veers back toward the boat about a foot beneath the surface and zooms right under us. We are all speechless. Finally, Weston breaks the silence. "Wow," he says, "that was *awesome!*"

I look at my watch. It's 6:30. I'm torn between trying another pass and doing the right thing, which involves making it home in time for dinner, baths, and a decent bedtime. Fish or go? Fish or go? A long moment passes while I weigh the options.

"Okay," I say, "I think we've had enough, you guys. We've hooked two kings and we have a great fish in the boat to take home. Let's pack it in."

"But Dad," Skyla says, "they just started biting. One more pass. Please? I would be so stoked if we had two. *Please?*"

"Yeah," Weston adds, "*stoked.*"

Who could argue with that? It's still officially summer, after all. And we have months of decent bedtimes ahead of us. I turn the boat back toward the point, put our gear in the water, and reach for my phone to call Stacy. We're going to be late.

AUTUMN

SOMETHING BRIGHT AND SHINY

Despite our concerted effort to limit the children's exposure to the global media-merchandising complex, Skyla's sense of style leans heavily toward the Disney princess look. Which is to say, glittery, shiny, and pink. Or what she calls *fancy*. Of the hundreds of anglers fishing the Sound on any given day, it's a good bet that I'm the only one whose partner is sporting a rhinestone tiara, polka-dot pouf skirt, and pink leggings, along with her rubber fishing boots and life jacket.

And, of course, what princess wants to be seen with a shabbily dressed peasant? "Here, Daddy," she says as we're packing lunch, "I made you a lucky fishing necklace like mine." It's a sparkling string of neon-pink fishing lures, each designed to attract fish by spinning on iridescent Mylar wings. These, though, have attracted a six-year-old girl. I found them in a box of gear left over from my guiding days in Alaska and gave them to Skyla last year. Now the gaudy lures belong to me once more. She slips the necklace over my head, adjusts it so that the biggest and shiniest lures hang in front, and smiles with satisfaction.

Feeling a little self-conscious, I zip up my fleece sweater to cover the new jewelry, but Skyla insists, "No, Dad, it has to be on the *out-side* or it won't work."

Fishing has been lousy. The kings have come and gone, and the usual wave of migratory silver salmon has not yet appeared in the Sound. It's difficult to say whether they're late, or not coming. They should be here by now. Typically, our silvers show up in early September on their way from the open ocean to spawning streams. As they move through the Sound, they feed aggressively and provide a bountiful fishery.

Some years, though, the silvers remain in the ocean until they're ready to spawn and then race through our inland sea without biting. One day the ocean fishing is red hot, and then the fish disappear for a week or so, only to magically reappear in the rivers without ever having shown themselves in the Sound. This is generally blamed on lack of rain, but we've had plenty. Nobody knows what's going on this year. Most of my fishing friends have either given up or headed to the coastal bays for the bigger and more abundant silvers out there. And I've been busy trying to catch up on house chores, wood stacking, and writing work, all of which are still suffering the neglect of king season. I haven't been on the water much lately.

But today, Skyla and I are going fishing. Just the two of us. Her school is closed for teacher conferences, a perfect excuse for me to take the day off as well. The gorgeous weather we've had the last few days renews my hope for Indian summer. Maybe the wood I left out will dry after all. The vine maples on the hillsides have already turned their luminous red, and a few pale alder leaves flutter to the ground each day, but everything else is holding on to deep, summer-green foliage. It hardly feels like fall.

With no one around on a weekday to protest, I decide to poach the neighborhood boat ramp. We put the boat in the water and cruise out into open water, puttering along to avoid rocking the moored boats with our wake. To the west, there's bustling activity on the Suquamish waterfront, a reservation town brought back to economic life, as so many are, by a flourishing casino. Clearly, the Great Recession has not put a damper on gambling. If anything, business at the casino has grown, and any time you happen to drive by, day or night, the six-story parking structure is full.

The Suquamish tribe still faces plenty of the same old challenges plaguing reservations everywhere, but it's now the third-largest employer in the county, and tribe members who once left to find work are returning home. Flexing newfound economic muscle, the tribe is actively expanding its business holdings and, in keeping with a timeless tradition of generosity, supporting a wide range of non-profit organizations throughout the region. The architectural beauty of their towering new cultural center, perched on a bluff above the water, bears witness to a new kind of pride and prosperity.

Just six miles south of here, in 1792, Captain Vancouver and Peter Puget dropped anchor and made the first contact between Europeans and Northwestern Native Americans. It seems doubtful that anyone standing on the beach that day could have imagined what this brief encounter would mean for their descendants. By 1855, with a tidal wave of white settlers and missionaries surging toward the West Coast, and fearing a war his people could not win, the great Suquamish leader, Chief Se'ahl (after whom the city of Seattle, at least in an Anglicized spelling, was named) signed the Treaty of Point Elliott, giving up most of the tribe's land in exchange for the security of promised health care, education, and fishing and hunting rights.

It's hard to fish these waters and not think about history. There is a thrill to closing my eyes and imagining the hillsides and beaches without houses, the water before 100 years of abuse. A time when the only manmade structures were the shed-roofed cedar long houses of Chief Se'ahl's people, and the sea held an abundance we cannot even begin to imagine today. Poet and novelist Jim Harrison writes that when missionaries headed west to save Native American souls, it was "the reverse of what it should have been." Amen.

Are we, the descendants of foreign invaders, a human version of the English ivy, European bindweed, and Himalaya blackberries that are now displacing native plants and taking over the landscape? *Noxious weeds*, the state calls them. *Invasive species.* In my case, I suppose, the plant would be Japanese knotweed.

But a six-year-old girl need not be concerned with such things. Our mission today is to find a silver for Skyla somewhere in the vast, apparently fishless Sound. Wait. Check that. The goal is to have fun, and if we catch a fish, we'll consider it a bonus. That's it.

To enhance our chances for said bonus, we'll fish bait today. Skyla reaches into the cooler and hands me a couple of six-inch herring that I brined overnight to toughen them up. I draw a sharp knife at a 45-degree angle behind their heads, creating a beveled leading edge so the bait will spin in the water like a drill bit.

There's a light breeze out of the southwest, just enough to feather the water's surface and remind me that somewhere out there, weather's brewing. If Indian summer's coming, it won't be anytime soon. We'll have rain by tomorrow. For now, we'll fish in our shirtsleeves and enjoy the sun on our arms. But I have to remember to tarp the firewood stacks tonight.

Whenever we get in the boat, Skyla eats like we might run out of food any minute. Today is no exception. We eat salty, oily strips of smoked king; small, tart apples from our tree; extra-sharp cheddar; crackers; chocolate chip cookies. Long after I'm full, Skyla continues to dip into our lunch box, chattering away while building elaborate creations on crackers, which she consumes with relish. She licks her fingers and wipes them on her polka-dot skirt. Maybe she's just tired from adjusting to her new school routines, but her usual predator instinct is muted today. Or maybe it's me. After king season ends, if it's been a good one and the freezer's full, I tend to fish with much less focus and intensity. We are a pair of kick-back fishermen today, just taking it easy.

"Hey," she says, pointing to the west, "that's where we saw the porpoises, isn't it?" I'm amazed at her memory and awareness of place. She scans the water hopefully for a repeat performance, and seeing nothing, tips her head back and stares up into the sky, a faint smile on her face. She spends a long time leaning over the gunwale, creasing the water's surface with her index finger, lost in her own private daydreams, hopes, and fears. What does she think about in these quiet moments?

Ever since she was a toddler, Skyla has always been helpful and hardworking. She seems to have an innate sense of responsibility, which grew more intense with the birth of her little brother. She has also developed a personal code of conduct that involves trying to maintain a stiff upper lip, complaining very little, and keeping her own counsel. She doesn't like anyone to see her cry. Where does this come from? I worry sometimes that the burden of responsibility – of being grown up at such an early age – might be too much weight for her slender shoulders. Though I am comforted by her day-to-day joy and enthusiasm, I often wonder what goes on in her mind. "What's up, bud?" I ask. "Nothing, Daddy," she replies in a dreamy voice. "I'm just looking for jellyfish."

She spots something way off in the distance and we slowly troll our way toward it to investigate. A young harbor seal has hauled out on a floating log. I expect it to dive when we approach, but the seal stays put, holding its head and tail high above the water and following us with its eyes. We circle around even closer. I think: *If we hook a fish now, the seal will grab it before we can do anything.* I have to fight my natural inclination to head the other way immediately.

"Dad, did you bring the camera?" Skyla asks. "It's in the box there," I say, "but the seal's going to take off before we get close enough for a picture." There I go, managing expectations again. I should know better. She opens the box, digs around, and finds our little point-and-shoot. We're going to have to get a lot closer for a decent picture. I circle back around again, the seal swiveling its head to follow our progress, and pull the boat in tighter. The seal does not take off. Skyla snaps photos as we turn, taking seal portraits at point-blank range. I could almost reach out and pet it. Finally, we decide to leave the seal undisturbed and go back to our fishing. "I can't wait to show these pictures to Mom and Weston," she says. "They won't believe how close we got." *I* can't believe how close we got.

With the excitement over, Skyla dozes in her seat. I put fresh bait on the hooks and troll in a wandering zigzag toward a row of houses built so low they appear to be rising out of the water. When we reach the sand spit, I turn to run along the shore just outside the mooring buoys. This is one of Smarty's favorite spots, and I can almost hear him saying *Fish those buoys on an outgoing.* It feels good to have a plan. When we reach the last buoy, I turn out to avoid the shoal, and Skyla's rod jerks down, bending deep into its cork handle.

"Skyla!" I shout, "Wake up. You have a fish on!" She jumps up, startled and bleary-eyed, but regains her senses quickly. I hand her the rod and there's a bright flash of silver way out behind the boat.

"Dad," she says, "you have to help me!" But I can see that she's managing on her own. I stop myself from taking the rod and instead place one hand above hers for support, then let her go. "Okay," I say, "are you alright?" "Yeah," she answers through clenched teeth, "I think so." The fish leaps high in the air, throwing a spray of water drops sparkling into the sunlight, and then suddenly reverses direction. The line goes slack.

"He's gone, Dad," she says, "I lost him." Her shoulders collapse. The loose belly of line shoots off to the right. "Reel fast," I say, "keep reeling."

Somehow, when she catches up with all the slack, her fish is still there. And Skyla is in full control of the situation now, pulling back and reeling down to gain line. I cut the motor, bring the other line in, and we're clear. The fish circles the boat, teetering a bit but still strong. I take the net in one hand and reach back to help Skyla lift the rod tip with the other, skidding the fish across the surface and into the net.

"Dad, it's my first salmon!" she says with a little victory jump.

"We've caught lots of other salmon," I say.

"Not by myself."

She has a point. This bright, shiny, six-pound silver does mean more than even the big kings we've fought together. I've learned something new about Skyla today, and caught a brief glimpse into her wholly self-sufficient future. Even more important, I think she has, too.

Skyla rinses the net and puts it away, sets her rod back in the holder and gets the bait. She watches carefully while I make the beveled cuts and rig the herring. Then we lower our lines, and we're fishing again. "Just think, sweetie," I say, half joking, "pretty soon you'll be able to come out and run the boat and fish all by yourself." She thinks about this for a while, then says, "Yeah, but I would still want you to come with me to keep me company." I hope she's right.

We fish through most of the falling tide without a bite. As we troll along, Skyla keeps getting up, going to the bow, and lifting the lid of the fish box to peer in at her catch. I remember doing the exact same thing as a kid, the thrill of having that fish in there, never tiring of looking at it. We cut back along the buoys, pulling our baits through the spot where we hooked our fish, but it seems empty now. If we fish any longer, the low tide will leave the ramp high and dry, and we won't be able to get the boat on the trailer. It's time to go.

Surprisingly, Skyla doesn't protest. She reels her line up by herself and bustles around the boat helping me put everything away, stopping only to peek into the fish box one more time. "Will Mom and Weston be home when we get there?" she asks. "Yes," I say. "Good...I can't wait to show them my fish and the seal pictures."

My tide calculations are not entirely correct. When we get to the ramp, it's already out of the water, the end of the exposed concrete slab hanging a foot above the surface. This isn't going to be easy. I back the trailer down and Skyla shouts when the wheels are at the very edge. I'm thinking we're going to have to wait for the tide to come in when Smarty pulls up in his boat, ties it to the dock and jumps out to help. As we work to winch the boat up onto the trailer, he keeps glancing at me and then looking away. Strange. But we're busy enough that I don't pay it much attention.

The minute we have the boat loaded and secured, Skyla runs up from the beach. "David!" she calls, "I caught a silver all by myself! Do you want to see it?" I lift the box over the bow and set it on the ground. She opens the lid with a flourish. "Wow! That's a good one," Smarty says. Skyla beams. Then Smarty looks at me again out of the corner of his eye and looks away when I notice.

I strap the boat down, get Skyla another snack, climb into the car, and start driving across the parking lot. Smarty jogs ahead to open the gate for us, and stands aside as we pass through. When I slow down to thank him, he leans toward my open window and says, "*Nice* necklace, dude." Fifty yards up the road I look in the rearview mirror and he's still doubled over with laughter.

Actually, I think it *is* a pretty nice necklace. Hell, it works. As long as you wear it on the outside.

Tomorrow night, Skyla will whisk crushed garlic, dill, sea salt and a dash of lemon juice into olive oil to marinate the fillets. We'll sear the fish in a hot pan to crisp the skin, then put it into a pre-heated oven for four more minutes. When it's done, she will serve her fish to a gathering of relatives from the East Coast and bask in the glory of effusive praise and cleaned plates. She will show them pictures of her fish and a baby seal. And I don't know who will be prouder, her or me.

BLACKBERRIES

Maybe it's the early rain, which softened the ripe berries, or a hectic back-to-school schedule filled with soccer practice and swimming lessons, but our usual enthusiasm for blackberry picking is lagging this year. We just can't seem to get going. The berries may be a little watery, but there are plenty of good ones mixed in, especially during the windows of sunny weather that open between storms. If we don't get on it soon, we'll kick ourselves in January, when frozen blackberries bring bright fall flavor to our muffins, yogurt, and oatmeal. And winter will surely feel longer and duller without a few blackberry crisps to lighten the mood.

Actually, I know why we haven't been out picking, but I've been slow to acknowledge it: We miss Grandma Karen. After a long illness, my stepmother passed away early this summer, and I guess it's only hitting us now.

Karen was the Blackberry Queen; at her insistence, she and my dad always timed their visits to be here at the peak of picking season. Even as her health declined, Karen harvested relentlessly, somehow finding the strength to fill baskets and bins long after everyone else had run out of steam. Then she would turn our kitchen counter into her production line, with blackberries moving along through separate sorting, rinsing, and drying stations. Finally, the berries went onto cookie sheets to freeze so they wouldn't stick together, and once solid, we rolled them into freezer bags. Last year, Grandma Karen's blackberries lasted us through February, and we thought of her every time we pulled a handful from the freezer. Berry picking without her just won't feel right. But it's something we need to get through.

After an unusually heavy September rain last week, a high-pressure ridge over the Cascades brought us four days of warm, dry weather. This morning, we woke to foghorns bellowing from the shipping lanes and spooky, floating skeins of mist drifting through the trees. The ridge is breaking down, allowing more ocean air into the Sound each night. The satellite shows an ominous swirl of dense clouds over the Pacific shifting shoreward. This afternoon might be the last sunshine for a while, and even if the rain holds off, we understand the odds favor wet over dry from here on out.

Everywhere around us, the sense of urgency grows: small, darting Douglas squirrels quit their summer chases to dig holes and store food; birds of all kinds gorge on blackberries, packing on fat for long journeys abroad or leaner times at home. Our Pacific flycatchers, their offspring grown, have abandoned the nest, and it sits empty in the awning above our deck. Last night, the evening air came alive with thousands of flying termites – Where are the flycatchers when you need them? – leaving the woods in search of new winter nests. If we're going to pick blackberries, now is the time.

There is no secret to finding blackberries on the Island. They're everywhere. Most roads, including ours, suffer from the ever-encroaching Himalaya blackberry vines, which need to be beaten back on a weekly basis. Any untended open space is quickly covered in blackberry barbed wire; abandoned buildings collapse under the burden of vines. The invasive Himalayas have become a Western version of the South's dreaded house-eating kudzu. Clearing these tenacious non-natives requires a light tractor at best and in extreme cases a diesel-powered implement of destruction called a chain-flail-er, which is exactly what it sounds like. More recently, enterprising farmers have been renting out herds of goats to devour the perva-sive brambles. With any method of control, though, there seems to be one simple truth: You can't stop Himalayas; you can only hope to contain them. Luther Burbank, the pioneering horticulturist, made many great contributions to American agriculture, but the import-ing and release of a blackberry he called Himalaya Giant was not his finest hour.

As the Himalayas flourish, our native, trailing-vine blackberries get tougher to come by each year. Like the Olympia oyster and native littleneck clam, they simply cannot compete with more aggressive, faster-growing imports. We rarely find enough of the small, tart, trailing-vine berries to make the effort worthwhile. There is, how-ever, another, more desirable non-native species here. The cutleaf blackberry's lacy, deeply serrated foliage is more beautiful, and its fragrant fruit tastier, than those of the Himalaya. Cutleaf berries are firmer when ripe, more resistant to rain, less prone to mold, and hold their shape better for freezing and baking. Their intense, tart-sweet flavor is also more complex and elegant. These are the berries Grandma Karen valued most.

Cutleaf vines don't fare much better than their native cousins when pitted against the potent Himalayas. Fortunately, a few cut-leaf strongholds remain nearby. Our favorite patch lies in an open field bordering a small bay at the south end of the Island. The cut-leaf vines grow in haystack-sized clumps, evenly spaced throughout the grassy meadow, as though someone had planted them on pur-pose for harvest. A few Himalayas are creeping in along the roadside ditch, but for now, the open country belongs to cutleafs.

The sun breaks through just as we arrive. Steam rises off the road. Our heavy jeans and sweatshirts, worn as protection against thorns, feel too hot within minutes.

But serious blackberry harvesting requires hand-to-hand combat with the vines; picking in shorts and T-shirts would be a bloodbath. Better to sweat than bleed. We cross into the meadow, breathing humid air filled with the sweetness of ripe berries.

Stacy and Skyla head to the far side, where a long hedgerow of cutleaf plants borders the bay. Weston and I make it about halfway across, then, following his lead, I veer toward the nearest clump of freestanding vines. "Ripe ones, Dad. See, look?" he says, dragging me by the hand toward his discovery. The world, or at least our awareness of it, shrinks to the vines, thorns, and berries directly in front of us, and we begin picking in earnest. An equal mix of green, moldy and ripe berries hang together in clumps, so we have to be selective. It's slow going, but gradually my basket fills. As usual, there are bigger, more perfect berries just beyond my reach. I remember telling Karen last year that we'd bring a ladder next time and really get after it.

I can't say my relationship with my stepmother was perfect. As kids, my brother and I spent the school year with our mom and summers with our dad and Karen. The transitions were never easy. We struggled with Karen over all the usual step-family issues, exacerbated by my teenage moodiness and the inevitable comparisons to our "real" mom. We wanted warm and fuzzy, and Karen seemed too critical and cool. But as we grew older, she softened – or maybe we did – and we began to see the efforts she made to reach out to us. Those efforts may have been there all along, but it took years for us to notice.

Weston stands behind me pointing to berry clusters I can't see from inside the "stickerbushes." From time to time, when I glance down to drop another berry into my basket, I see a small hand grabbing a handful and withdrawing. The more I pick, the lighter my basket becomes. Eventually, he gets his fill and wanders off in search of berries low enough to pick by himself.

"Dad," Weston calls from the other side of the brambles, "I, I... need help." I extricate myself from the snagging thorns, set my basket down and start looking for him. "I'm stuck," he says when I find him. One thick, barbed stalk holds the back of his sweatshirt, and another grips his pants below both knees. Yet another is snarled in his hair. But none have pierced his skin. He's scratched up a little, and currently immobilized, but not hurt. "What are you doing way back in here?" I ask while slowly and carefully pulling thorns from his clothes. He points upward and deeper into the thicket. "Look at those dandies," he whispers.

Dark purple stains cover his fingers, lips, and a good portion of his face. He has purple handprints smeared across the front of his sweatshirt and anywhere else he could reach. And yet his basket is empty. "Where are all your berries?" With great pride, he pats his belly, shrugs, and smiles.

Fortunately for us, the girls picked up our slack. They have a whole flat of gorgeous, plump blackberries, plus another large basketful. The boys have Weston's full stomach and purple hands, and the few berries he left in my basket. No thanks to us, the family has made a good haul. If the weather holds, we could still end up with enough berries to last through winter. Or maybe I will drag the ladder down here and really get after it. But for now, we're happy to call it a day and proud of our – Stacy and Skyla's, that is – harvest. Grandma Karen would approve.

Tonight, I will call my mom and ask for her blackberry pie recipe. We'll freeze most of what we picked, but something about Weston's purple fingers has me thinking of the flaky, slightly salty crust and tangy filling I remember from my own childhood.

I need to call my dad too. We've talked more over the past few months than we have since I was a kid, and I look forward to checking in with him every few days. Mostly we keep it light, chatting about the kids' soccer games, his latest round of golf, or recipes for smoked salmon brine. Sometimes he helps me with long-distance advice on fixing the leaky skylight or troubleshooting my computer. It's good for both of us. Today, I want to tell him about our blackberry picking, but I wonder if it might be painful for him to hear, or for me to say.

We walk back to the car quietly. I'm not sure if the kids consciously miss their grandmother or if it's more elusive than that, but I think we all feel better for having come out to pick today. And I know we'll remember Grandma Karen whenever we drop frozen blackberries into our oatmeal or bake a crisp this winter. Maybe by then we'll find it easier to talk about missing her.

A faint sound, like barking dogs in the distance, breaks the silence. Canadian geese. We look toward the horizon, searching the open sky between tall cedars. And then, finally, a ragged wedge of tiny specks appears, pointed south toward the winter warmth of California rice fields. I am reminded of Ted Leeson's brilliant observation that it is really we, the earthbound, who are moving, while geese "take to altitudes to stay in one place, not migrating, but hovering, while the equinoctial tilting of the earth rocks the poles back and forth beneath them." As our northern hemisphere careens into winter shadows – taking us along with it – the geese remain forever the perfect distance from the sun. "Their seasonal appearance," Leeson writes, "denotes your passing, not their own."

LIGHT IN THE FOREST

Behold the world's greatest mushroom hunter: Three feet, two inches tall. Agile. Enthusiastic. Energetic. Built to clamber over fallen logs and slide under brambles. Undaunted by steep terrain or dense brush. Ecstatic over mud, rain, puddles, and any opportunity to get dirty. Turns out, at three years old, Weston is the perfect chanterelle-picking partner.

Monday morning, deep into the autumn rainy season. Skyla's at school, Stacy's in the shop building light fixtures, and Weston and I are discussing our plans for the day over breakfast.

"We could play dinosaurs," he says hopefully.

"We play dinosaurs every day," I say.

"But you could be *Tyrannosaurus rex* this time," he says, upping the ante.

"Nah, let's go do something new today," I tell him.

"We could play dinosaur wrestling, or do my dinosaur puzzle."

"Why don't we take a little hike and see if we can find some chanterelles."

"Okay! Um...what are chantrulls?"

Some years, after the first big autumn rains, we're treated to a stretch of crisp, clear nights and warm, blue-sky days. Bigleaf maples bathe the woods behind our house in golden-yellow light, and the scent of late-ripening blackberries hangs in the air. Indian summer, when it happens here, feels like an extravagance, a gift we savor even more than the bright, overhead sun of high summer. But this is not one of those years.

Instead, an endless procession of storms has lined up across the Pacific all the way to Hawaii. As they push toward us, a new front arrives with heavy rain and wind every two or three days and lasts pretty much until the next one. This will be a year when anything – firewood, life jackets, deck chair cushions – left outside in October won't dry out until May. Mold spores throughout the region rejoice.

The weather service is calling for a brief break between storms this morning. Which means it's only going to drizzle for a few hours before the next downpour. As we put on our boots and rain gear, I tell Weston we'll get off the trail and bust brush, searching for bright flashes of ruffled gold on the dark forest floor. "Will we find any?" he asks. I tell him I'm not sure, that they're hard to see, that we're going to a new place and you just never know. More expectation management. "It'll be like a treasure hunt," I say, "and we'll just have fun searching around in the woods. Okay?"

Just up the road from our house there's a small piece of public forest that looks ideal for chanterelles. I've driven past it hundreds of times, but until recently I've never thought to check there. Maybe it just seems too close to home to be any good. When we drive into the small parking area, massive second-growth firs block the already muted October light, towering above a thick lower story of black huckleberry, salal, Oregon grape, and sword ferns. Very little alder, maple, or bracken fern. Perfect.

More importantly, this section of forest has yet to be attacked by the rapidly spreading invasive weeds that are choking out native foliage all over the Island. English ivy and field bindweed – wild morning glory – strangle trees and outcompete natural ground cover in their race to dominate the woods. Japanese knotweed, with its giant leaves and savagely fast growth rate, shades and obliterates all other plants. The invaders come with beautiful names and destructive habits. Creeping buttercup, milk thistle, English holly, Queen Anne's lace, herb Robert (also known as stinky Bob), and, of course, the ubiquitous Himalaya blackberry now cover our landscape. Some were imported by gardeners, others spread accidentally, but they're all wreaking havoc on our forest ecosystems. Invasive plants are easy to ignore, too, until you return to a favorite old chanterelle spot, see ivy on the tree trunks, and know that the mushrooms are gone. If Chief Se'ahl could see the forest here today, I doubt he'd recognize it.

But this little patch of woods seems perfect. The one thing I know for sure about chanterelles, though, is this: They only grow where it looks right, but not every place that looks right has chanterelles. Clearly, there are mysterious factors – soil chemistry, microclimates, drainage patterns – that determine chanterelle growth, yet remain invisible to me. Which is why I'm never sure I'm going to find any until I actually find them.

I unbuckle Weston from his car seat and he hits the ground running. While I stuff a bag in my pocket, grab a water bottle, and make sure I'm loaded with snacks, he's already scurrying through the underbrush around the gravel parking space. "Dad," he calls from beneath a thick stand of salal, "I found one. I found a chantrull, come here." It's going to be a long day. "Come on, buddy, let's go up the trail a ways and get farther in before we start looking," I say. "No," he says, "Come here first."

I breathe in deeply and hear myself let out a long sigh. "Weston, we're still in the *parking lot*...come on."

"Dad, may I please...you come here?" He thinks I'm refusing to join him because he forgot his manners. Now that he's used the magic word, I have no choice. I can see his boots, but the brush is so thick I can't get to him. Another big sigh and I'm on my stomach, crawling to meet him. And there, in front of where he's crouched, not 10 feet from the car, is a perfect, big, beautiful, golden chanterelle. Behind it, I see another, smaller crown poking up through the fir needles, and beyond that, several more.

I show him how to rock the mushroom back and forth while lifting it to pull it from the ground. When he succeeds, he hands me his prize in triumph. We quickly put half a dozen into our bag, he crouching and I lying on my belly in the wet dirt. So much for managing expectations. I peel one apart, showing him the fibrous, chicken-breast texture, and he sniffs the distinctive vanilla-apricot scent. We high-five and grin stupidly at each other, and then, after a thorough search of the surrounding area, crawl back out and hit the trail leading deeper into the forest. "Dad," Weston says, "Let's hold hands and run real fast."

We don't run very far, for two reasons: one, I'm out of breath, and two, Weston skids to a stop every 10 feet to examine fallen leaves, stomp through mud puddles, and throw fir cones. A quarter-mile in, we leave the trail and start searching again. We thrash through underbrush, pulling spider webs off our faces and tripping over blackberry vines. I worry the terrain might be too rough for Weston, but he's hanging in there. And he's having a whale of a time. "Can stickerbushes stop *Tyrannosaurus rex*? No! T-Rex can go anywhere!" he yells, adding a passionate roar for emphasis.

After tromping along in full dino-mode for some distance, he says, "Dad, can I eat these black huckleberries?" We have a family rule that before the kids eat anything they find in the woods, they have to ask and show it to us, no matter how sure they are. I look at the clump of shiny black berries he's eyeballing and tell him to go ahead. Out of the corner of my eye, I watch as he stretches up on tippy-toes to eat them off the branch without using his hands. He gets a mouthful, then pulls away, stripping berries from the branch. When he catches me watching, he smiles and laughs with purple berry juice dripping down his chin. We continue deeper into the woods without a word.

My eyes are focused on the ground now, searching. As often happens, I lose all track of time and space. A week ago, in another spot nearby, I snapped out of my chanterelle trance realizing that not only had I lost track, I was lost, period. A mile from the house on an island full of people and homes, I felt the panic of complete disorientation. I had thought I was working my way back toward the trail, searching for mushrooms as I went, when I came to a creek bed I'd never seen before. I stopped, looked around, and a creeping dread came over me. The trees and brush looked exactly the same in every direction, and when I tried to determine which way I'd come, I could not find a trace of my passage anywhere.

For a master plan, I decided to walk 100 steps in several different directions. If I didn't see anything that looked familiar, I'd retrace my steps to where I first realized I was lost. Three directions out and back, and it all looked the same. And it was getting dark fast. Just as I was plotting some new, equally lame strategy, the setting sun broke through the clouds, and I was saved with a bearing point. Two hundred yards in the direction I hadn't taken, but which I now knew was south, I hit the trail and jogged back to the car, relieved.

At dinner that night, I told Stacy and the kids about it and we laughed. But I kept thinking there must be some deeper meaning or lesson to be learned from getting lost in the woods so close to home in this era of suburban sprawl, cell phones, and GPS. Like carry a compass, dumb ass.

So, as Weston and I search our way through the brambles, I make a mental note to stay a little more in touch with reality and not get so absorbed in the hunt. Then, standing up from looking beneath a big clump of Oregon grape, I realize that I can no longer see or hear the little guy. "Weston?" I shout. Nothing. "Weston?" louder now. Still nothing. A panic far greater than I felt when I was lost rises in my chest. Small branches snap somewhere to my left. "I'm right here, Dad, I just have to climb over this..." Then a sharp cracking sound and the loud "Ooof!" of a body hitting the ground. Silence. The kind of dreadful post-thud, pre-cry silence every parent knows. I wait, and even worse, there is no crying. Fear surges through me, and I tear through the brush in a cold sweat. A new sound fills the forest now, quiet at first, then louder. Laughter. He's laughing. By the time I reach him, he's roaring with hilarity, lying on his back below the broken-off branch of a fallen maple.

"Hey," I say, trying to hide my fading distress, "What's so funny, bud?"

"Falling down in the forest is fun," he giggles, "because the moss is so soft it doesn't hurt."

I laugh with him and when I reach to lift him up, I let him pull me down instead. We lie on the moss looking up into the tall trees and the sky beyond. "Dad," he says, "May you please...I ride on your back for a while?" "Absolutely, buddy, absolutely."

After a short piggyback ride, I set him down in a likely-looking clearing and we start searching again. "Here's one," he says casually, as though he's been finding chanterelles his whole life. "And there's another one." He's so close to the ground, he's spotting them under ferns, around fallen logs, and in tight spots I can't even see. In a very short while, we have enough in the bag for dinner and then some. With each find, Weston wants to hold the chanterelle and look at it, and more than that, he wants to smell them, sniffing deeply and saying "They smell sweet!" (Actually, he says they "they *fell* sweet," which reminds me of yesterday in the grocery store checkout line, when he tried to tell everyone he had a very *sm*art daddy. Which reminds me I need to take him to see *Sm*arty sometime soon, just for a laugh. That joke never gets old.)

Now we're really in the chanterelles, and I decide we should keep picking. We can dry what we don't eat right away (the intensified flavor more than makes up for what you lose in texture), and there are always friends who could use a few. But I also have another motive:

I've already traded "mushroom futures" for an apple pie made by a neighbor who's both an unbelievable baker and a serious chanterelle lover. Stupid, perhaps, to trade something you don't have, but I couldn't resist that pie. Now, I'm not only in debt, but we've long since eaten the pie. It was delicious. This is an unexpected chance to make good.

When we've filled the bag and even stuffed a few extra chanterelles into our pockets, we stop and sit on a moss-covered log, eating pretzels and toasting our big score with the shared water bottle. A sharp drumming sound breaks the silence and we watch a pileated woodpecker pounding holes in an old fir stump, searching for lunch. "Is that a p-p-p-pie-laded woodpecker?" Weston asks, his almost-gone baby stutter making a brief return. Last year, we were concerned about the stammer; now, I think I'm going to miss it when it's gone.

Busting our way back to the trail, Weston says under his breath, "There aren't any bears 'round here," and again, louder, "There aren't any bears 'round here." I wonder if my panic earlier might be causing him some fear or stress. "There aren't any bears 'round here," he repeats, trying to convince himself, and then, "Are there, Dad?" I'm caught in a classic parenting dilemma. The chances of running into a bear here are infinitesimal. Microscopic. But not impossible. The odd bear does occasionally make its way onto the Island. What if I lie to assuage his fears and we actually run into one? What credibility would I have with him in the future? But I don't want to scare him, either. I compromise: "No, there aren't any bears around here. But if there were, they would be more scared of us than we are of them." I wait for a response while he digests the information. "Yeah," he says, finally. "They'd be more scared of us. That's funny. Can I look in the bag at the chantrulls again?"

At home, Weston is buoyant over our success. He insists on carrying the bag into the house "to show Mom," though the handles are too long and he's forced to hold his arms above his head to keep it from dragging. We spread the chanterelles out on the kitchen table, examining them and holding up the largest specimens to admire. Skyla comes in from school, and to her credit, especially for a six-year-old, hides her disappointment at missing out, and compliments Weston on the harvest. That her compliments fall something short of full enthusiasm goes unnoticed. I brush fir needles and bigger clumps of dirt off the mushrooms, and put the bulk of our haul into paper bags to be stored in the fridge.

We take the dozen or so Weston has selected for dinner to the sink and I quickly rinse away the remaining grime. Many chanterelle aficionados will recoil at this cleaning process, insisting as they do that washing the mushrooms in water removes flavor. But I just don't like eating dirt. And my uneducated taste buds can't detect any difference after a quick rinse anyway.

Now the possibilities are limitless. Should we sauté them in butter and scramble creamy farm eggs into the pan? There's crabmeat in the freezer, how about adding that and a little garlic, too? Or would that be too rich and decadent? What about a slow simmer with shallots and white wine? I briefly consider a stir fry, but decide that wouldn't be giving the mushrooms enough respect. Finally, Stacy, who appreciates chanterelles most of all, comes to the rescue.

She's already roasting a chicken with rosemary and garlic for dinner and feels the chanterelles would be best served over creamy polenta, next to the sweet, late beets and sautéed greens from the garden. When the bird comes out of the oven and the polenta has thickened, I quarter the mushrooms the long way and drop them into a hot, dry pan. As they sizzle, releasing their fragrant moisture, I add a chunk of butter and a little crushed garlic. And before the "sauce" can evaporate, I pour the contents of the pan over each serving of steaming cornmeal pudding. An incredible, savory aroma fills the kitchen.

The flavors are even better. There's the warm, comforting chicken with crispy, garlic-scented skin. The mineral sweetness of cold-weather beets and their contrasting, slightly bitter greens. The hearty, creamy cornmeal texture of polenta...and, of course, the chanterelles: a mild, earthy taste of the forest with natural buttery hints enhanced by the actual butter I added – distinctive, but much less assertive than shiitakes or portobellos. Nothing like grocery-store button mushrooms at all. Stacy can't wait, and picks hot chanterelle pieces directly from the pan with her fingers. Skyla gamely eats a few, although without much gusto.

"Weston," I say, "you're eating everything but the chanterelles; give 'em a try." He spears one with his fork and examines it closely. Sniffs it. And nibbles the tiniest corner before spitting it out with a frown. "Chantrulls...I say blech!" he says, already scooping a spoonful of chanterelle-free polenta into his mouth. Could there be a better chanterelle-picking partner? Finds and picks but doesn't eat the treasured harvest. Perfect.

Late at night, the pounding rain returns, driven from the south by a rising 30-knot gale. Drops pelt the bedroom windows like thrown gravel. Our brief intermission is over and the storm parade marches on. There's a long winter ahead, but I think we're ready for it. As I drift off to sleep, I dream of finding a dead bear in the woods behind our house. I am overcome by an urgent need to drag the carcass away before the kids come outside. Pulling frantically on one enormous, outstretched paw, I discover that the bear isn't dead after all, but sleeping. When he wakes, the bear is not more afraid of me than I am of him.

CONVERSATION WITH
A THREE-YEAR-OLD

Weston: Why are we outside in the middle of the night, Daddy?

Me: You have a little fever, bud. We're just trying to cool you off. Can you smell the clean air?

Weston: Queen? Like a girl king?

Me: No, clean, like fresh from the rain...can you see the rain coming down?

Weston: I'm not afraid of the dark.

Me: Okay, good. We can just leave the porch light off then.

Weston: Yeah, we don't need the porch light...Dad? I think we should turn on the porch light.

Me: Okay. There.

Weston: I'm not afraid of the dark.

Me: Hey, are you feeling better, bud?

Weston: Yes. Can we go shark fishing?

Me: Maybe this summer we can catch some dog sharks when we're salmon fishing...

Weston: Yeah, or a great white, or a mako, or a blacktip, or a tiger,
           or a whale shark...

Me: Probably just dog sharks, but you never know... You ready
           to go back inside?

Weston: I'm not afraid of the dark.

Me: Okay, you feel cooler now. Let's go up to bed. You ready?

Weston: Dad? The air smells sweet like candy.

LAST CHANCE

Sweeney already has his deer, a beautiful, thick-shouldered, forked-horn he shot on the first day of the season. This little venison-craving piggy has none. In an obvious attempt to reduce the amount of meat I'm going to "borrow" this winter, Sweeney suggests we hunt the last day of the season together. And since he's already tagged out, I will be doing all the shooting. Sounds good to me. Two sets of eyes and ears beat one, and if nothing else, it'll be a good excuse to hang out together and spend some time in the woods. With another storm headed our way, conditions couldn't be better. We should get our deer.

Fact is, I haven't been deer hunting in more than 20 years. Last time I went, my buddy, Nate, and I spent a foggy afternoon on a steep coastal hillside glassing the valley below. Late in the day, when the fog cleared, we spotted two does and a nice buck. Between us and the deer lay 200 yards of near-vertical, blackberry-covered slope, littered with old stumps and blowdowns. I put the crosshairs on the buck's shoulder, steadied my breath...and couldn't squeeze the trigger. I'm not sure why. The rough terrain provided a good excuse – neither of us wanted to haul a deer up that hill, especially in the dark – but there was something else going on. I just didn't feel like killing a large animal anymore.

In the years since, though, my taste for venison has grown. And grown. To the point where my mouth waters while chasing tame local deer from our garden and I feel hunger pangs at the sight of road kill on the highway. Fortunately, I have enough friends who are hunters that I can usually beg, grovel, and trade for deer meat to take the edge off my craving. I have traded everything from smoked salmon and chanterelles to firewood and even writing for deer.

I'm not picky, either. I like it all. The pungent gaminess of our small, forest-dwelling western Washington blacktails; the tangy sage flavor of high-desert mule deer; the tender, marbled flesh of wheat-field whitetails...to me, it's all good. We marinate thick rump steaks in olive oil, garlic, and rosemary, then sear them rare in a hot cast-iron pan. Scraps – usually labeled "stew meat" – are never wasted on stew in our house, but instead skewered and quickly charred over white-hot coals. Sausage patties, well-seasoned and mixed with pork fat and apples, have become our favorite breakfast meat. And the coveted, melt-in-your mouth backstrap that nobody ever wants to part with...well, the only problem is, nobody ever wants to part with it.

My feelings about killing a deer are changing. Not back to the pure bloodlust I felt when I was younger, or because of my current yearning for venison, but somehow connected to having children. Part of it is a concern for our health that has grown with our awareness of the antibiotics and growth hormones used in industrial meat production. But there's also a sense that we, as carnivores, should participate – at least on some level – in procuring the meat we eat. There's really only one solution: Go get my own deer.

Two hours before dawn, Sweeney and I pull into a gas station convenience store for coffee. The rising wind swirls dry leaves through the halo of white fluorescent glare around the pumps. A neon sign in the window advertises BEER BAIT AMMO, and the parking lot bustles with hunters packing two of the three items out to their trucks by the case. Nobody's going fishing, either. Business is booming, and with good reason – we are just outside a vast private forest that produces one of the highest deer harvest rates in western Washington. The timber company that owns the land manages it for maximum lumber production, with a byproduct of exceptionally robust deer numbers. As a gesture of goodwill – or shrewd public relations – they open this parcel to the public during deer season, and hunters respond by converging en masse. We won't be alone in the woods today.

When I express some concern about the Alcohol Tobacco and Firearms crowd running through the forest fully locked and loaded, Sweeney says it actually works in our favor. "With all the people and this wind, the deer'll have to keep moving. We should see a lot of deer." I pull on my fluorescent orange vinyl "hunter safety" vest in the parking lot, wishing it was Kevlar.

We turn off the paved road five miles beyond the gas station, pass through an open gate, and start up a winding, muddy two-track in pitch-black night. Sweeney stops to lock the hubs on his old black Chevy truck and gets back into the cab soaking wet. "Weather's perfect," he says, without irony. Worn-out wiper blades chatter across the windshield and I can hear wind whipping through the trees.

Halfway up the mountain as the truck crawls along in four-low, a big doe streaks through the headlights and disappears into a wall of sapling firs. A few minutes later, another deer, possibly a spike, bounds across the road. A good sign, but the reprod – reproduction timber – planted along the road for future harvest is too thick to hunt. Hell, you couldn't walk through it sideways. The density of wrist-thick trunks and brushy foliage, grown in typical monoculture style, is no accident. It's designed to block sunlight and suppress the growth of any less profitable vegetation. During hunting season, reprod also provides ideal refuge for the deer. Shooting time won't start for another half hour, so we continue up the increasingly steep road. It could be the convenience-store coffee, but my heart's beating a little faster now.

We park the truck on the edge of an apocalyptic landscape. The clear-cut stretches out below us, 100 acres of treeless earth, the ground shredded by heavy equipment and littered with piles of stumps, root wads, and branches waiting to be burned. To anyone other than a deer hunter (or timber corporation accountant) it would be an atrocity...but today, we're looking for deer, not beauty. And this is prime deer habitat. The ravaged ground, newly open to the sun, grows thick with young shrubs and tender, sweet grass. A deer feedlot. Without trees to obscure our view, we have clear sight lines all the way across.

We pick our way through discarded slash, tripping and sliding, to an enormous stump we can lean against and have a commanding view. The rain has quit, but the icy north wind is rising. Sweeney starts glassing from the right edge, sweeping his binoculars slowly in a grid pattern. I have the rifle cradled in my lap and scan with naked eyes from the left side, searching for movement. I catch a brief flicker of something – an ear? A tail? – way down on the far edge where the uncut timber starts. I try to focus, squinting my eyes until I spot the blue and black Stellar's jay hopping along a fallen log.

Gradually, a deep chill sets in, the kind you only get from sitting on cold ground for a long time without moving. The wind blows harder, trees sway and thrash, and yet we see no sign of deer. They should be here, seeking fuel to keep warm, or moving through ahead of the lunatic crowds. At some point, a lone doe steps cautiously out of the forest and picks her way through the slash. My pulse quickens. We watch for the buck who's surely following until it's apparent she's traveling alone. My excitement fades, and with it, the last of my warmth.

Rigor mortis sets in. When I try to stand up, my knees can barely unfold to climb the hillside and my lower back tingles as though any sudden movement might trigger a blowout. In this ossified state, slipping and crashing our way back to the truck, we stumble upon a big three-pointer bedded down behind a root wad. It leaps to its feet, looks directly at us, and calmly angles away through the brush. I'm so surprised, I never even unsling my rifle.

The buck reappears in a small clearing about 300 yards downslope, looks back over its shoulder, then slowly browses its way out of sight again. We hold still for a few moments, and without speaking, start working our way down. There are tracks in the loose dirt where he last appeared; calm, evenly spaced hoofprints, headed toward the creek bottom. We follow with as much stealth as we can muster, which means only a few dozen loudly snapped twigs and the occasional hissing call of "Hey, you see anything over there?"

But now, with prey nearby, I'm *hunting*, my senses taken over by a strange, heightened awareness of surroundings, sparked, perhaps, by latent predator instincts. I can smell wet moss growing on rocks along the stream. A pair of silver salmon spawning in a shallow tailout catches my attention. The bright, ruffled edge of a hidden chanterelle peeks out from under deer-trampled sword ferns. Half a hoofprint, barely visible, appears clearly to me in a muddy seam between rocks. When the wind shifts, I catch myself inhaling deeply, searching for a scent of prey with an olfactory sense no longer sharp enough to do the job.

My old friend Andy Landforce, renowned Oregon steelhead guide and a man more in touch with the natural world than any I've known, would track this deer until he caught up with it. When I was a kid, I followed Andy into the woods and watched him slowly, methodically chase down a buck, my skepticism shot down by the sharp crack of his rifle at the end of the stalk. I know it's possible. But not for us, not here. We stay with the tracks until they meander into impenetrable reprod, and unable to follow, we reluctantly give up the chase. This deer, at least today, has reached safe haven.

It's a long hike back. Uphill, rough, and no longer eased by the rush of adrenaline we had on the way down. By the time we reach the truck, I am sweat-soaked and chilled from the cold wind. "Man, that was a good hunt," Sweeney says, then adds, "but I guess you can't eat good hunting." We laugh. It feels good to climb into the truck and sit down. It feels even better when the engine warms up enough to turn on the heat. Maybe it just wasn't meant to be this year. Going out on the last day expecting to bring home a buck is a sure sign of either optimism or ignorance. And I think we've already established what kind of optimist I am.

The back way off the mountain is more a random collection of gaps between trees, monster potholes, and washboard turns than road. Around a sharp, descending bend, a clogged culvert overflowed during the last big rain, creating a nearly impassable washout. The road's too narrow to turn the truck around, so I walk ahead to guide Sweeney as he picks his way through the gullies and rubble. When our path resembles something close to a road again, I climb back in, and we rattle and bounce downhill through grainy, failing light. It's getting dark early these days.

Heat blasts from under the dashboard now, warming my feet and lulling me into a drowsy half sleep. We're already making plans for next year. We'll hunt together from Opening Day, really make a season of it. I wipe condensation off the side window and glance down an old, overgrown spur road. There's a nice forked-horn standing at the far end, head down, feeding on grass growing through the gravel. Maybe the season isn't over yet. "Did you see that?" I ask. "Yeah," Sweeney says, "but if I stop the truck, he'll take off."

"Okay," I say, "just keep going slow." Another 100 yards down the road, I grab the rifle, slide the door open and quietly roll out onto the muddy road. For some reason, "Ride of the Valkyries" thunders in my head. Sweeney keeps driving. Knowing the buck won't want to move toward the main road where the truck just passed, my plan is to drop below the road, work my way back toward the spur, and come up right where he was feeding.

Great plan. Only the hill below the road is a little steeper and the brush a lot thicker than it looked from up above. I step down into a mass of head-high salmonberry, trip over something and slide about thirty feet with thorns and branches tearing at me the whole way. On the upside, it's a relatively quiet fall. And I end up about where I wanted. So far, so good.

I regain my footing and attempt to bust brush silently back toward the spur road. It's not easy. I take one step, bend branches and pull vines off my clothes, then another. Somehow, no twigs snap, and I remain vertical. But the pace is agonizingly slow, and it's tough to quell the urge to hurry, to get there before the deer wanders away on its own. One step...pull blackberry thorns out of my neck... another step...pull blackberry thorns off my leg...

When I finally reach the base of the spur road, I pause to catch my breath and plot the quietest path up the steep slope. There isn't any kind of trail, but I can see a slight opening in the salal to my left, then a fern-covered clearing leading to a huge, rotten cedar log that angles up toward the road. From there, I should be able to see the deer.

I make it through the salal and shuffle up through the ferns. At the downhill end of the log, I lie on my belly and start a weak imitation of the Marine Corp training crawl, elbows in the mud and my rifle held up in front of me. When I reach the top end – the last of my cover – I roll onto my side to get some circulation back into my arms and calm myself.

I flick off the safety and come up over the end of the log, already raising the gun to my shoulder, and...he's gone. I scan the brush and dark hillside in every direction, already knowing I'm too late. There's a hollow feeling inside my chest where just moments before my heart was hammering. Was he really even there, or did I imagine the whole thing? I walk out to the main road in the murky light of late-autumn dusk.

Sweeney's waiting a quarter mile down. I get into the truck, and he starts for home. There's not much to say. The season is over.

The Sweeney house is filled with the delicious scent of slow-cooking venison. Mia has a magnificent pot roast from Sweeney's Opening Day deer just coming out of the oven, and I gratefully sit down to dinner. Maren and Laine talk about school and friends and basketball. Mia fills Sweeney in on the day's events. And I consume three helpings of succulent pot roast, mashing my potatoes into the braising liquid and cutting tender carrots with my fork.

"Why don't you take some of this deer home with you," Sweeney says. "We have plenty, really." I have to force myself to politely refuse. "Nah," I say, "you need the meat, keep it, we're good. Thanks, though." Looking relieved, he excuses himself and goes outside to unload the truck. I have another helping of pot roast.

On my drive home, I am haunted by the image of the buck standing there on the spur road. Next year, I tell myself. *Next year.*

It's late when I pull into our driveway. I'm so tired, I sit for a long moment, not moving, listening to the tick-tick of cooling engine metal. I reach into the backseat to grab my gear, and hidden under my jacket I find a stack of packages neatly wrapped in butcher paper. I switch the dome light on and read the labels written in Sweeney's hand: *Roast. Shoulder steaks. Sausage. Stew meat. Backstrap...*

Inside, Stacy is curled up on the couch by the woodstove, deeply immersed in the latest composting literature. "Well?" she says, looking up, "how was it? Did you bring home the bacon?" I'm not quite sure how to answer.

THE SIGNIFICANCE OF BIRDS III

Running the boat home from fishing up north, I spot a single white egret hunting through high-tide marsh grass along the shore. I cut the motor and drift, the silence echoing through calm evening air. The bird stands motionless, watching the water, then slowly lifts a foot and takes a cautious, halting step, illuminated by warm light. My San Francisco grandpa – the quiet, dignified man who fed my early obsession with fishing trips to Fort Point Pier and visits to Steinhart Aquarium – is checking in.

It's another of my mom's beliefs, formed by the sight of countless snowy egrets lining the road of her father's funeral procession. Perhaps it wasn't so unusual to see these birds along the Marin shoreline that day, and yet I have found comfort in the presence of egrets ever since. There is something in the egret's serene, almost ethereal presence that eases my natural skepticism.

My grandfather was an artist; a forager of spring fiddleheads and forest mushrooms; a poet who wrote a single, perfect haiku for every day he was held in the relocation camps. The day he was taken from his young family to another, distant prison camp, he wrote these words about his daughter, my mother:

I'm leaving/But the suntanned child/Doesn't know.

The last time I saw him, I was still a young boy. He was fading then and, I'm sure, aware that the end was near. I sat next to him in the darkened living room, the air scented with camphor and green tea, as we went through the treasured box of arrowheads and spear points he was leaving me. They were artifacts he'd found 35 years earlier while pacing back and forth behind the camp fence in Bismarck, North Dakota; a connection to the original foragers. I remember from that day, a small cowlick had sprung free from the back of his neatly slicked-down hair, a plume; feathery, white, ethereal. His transformation had already begun.

FIREWOOD III: PROCUREMENT

Windfall: An unexpected, unearned, or sudden gift, gain, or advantage.

"There's a madrona down on Lovgren," Stacy says, coming in the door after dropping Skyla off at school. I'm at the kitchen counter, blearily eating breakfast, trying to wake up. I'm only half paying attention, absorbed in thoughts of my full day ahead. There's a rapidly approaching work deadline, a phone conference at eleven o'clock, and I'm considering putting the boat in the water to fish the afternoon tide.

"There's a madrona down, and it's a big one," Stacy repeats, nearly shouting. Suddenly I remember hearing wind in the trees last night. Now it's starting to make sense. A big madrona? I gulp down the last of my cereal, throw the saws and cutting gear into the car, and hit the road. Along the way, I call to postpone my phone conference and try to calculate if I can still make my Friday work deadline. There's no way I'm passing up a madrona. I press down on the gas pedal, tormented by visions of wood poachers from all over the Island converging on "my" tree like iron filings to a magnet.

The tree is indeed a big madrona, lying across the road in a tangle of broken branches and leafy twigs. Better yet, it has fallen from an empty lot (no homeowners to deal with), and there's nobody else here yet. I can hardly believe my good fortune. Of course, there's the small matter of a severed power line dangling in its branches, but you can't get bogged down in details on the brink of a major score. There's a guy from the power company working from a cherry picker down the road. He says go ahead, they've already cut the electricity, but be careful around the wire anyway.

I duck through the smaller branches to mark the beefy lower limbs and telephone pole-thick trunk in 16-inch lengths with my marker stick and pruning saw. Then I fire up the big saw, a battle-scarred Stihl 36 with a brand-new 24-inch Oregon bar, and step in to start cutting. I remind myself to stay clear of the power line, and then decide I really ought to stand back and take a closer look at the whole tree. As my dad likes to say, *hurrying only makes bad things happen faster.* I need to slow down, check all the angles, and see where the pressure lies on the trunk. Almost every downed tree, no matter how straight it looks, is somehow sprung in one direction or another. Last thing I want to do is get the saw stuck in a pinching cut or get knocked on my ass by a sudden release of tension.

As I'm standing there with the saw idling in my hand, the first vulture arrives in a beater Ford pickup. "Hey," he calls over the rattling saw, trying to sound official, "This isn't your property, is it?" "No," I say, thinking, *Too late, sucker. Nice try.* But he's not giving up. "Well...is this your tree?" he asks, still attempting to bluff me out of the picture. "It is now," I say and turn to start cutting.

Two hours later I'm still cutting sections off the main trunk, and there's a nice stack of 16-inch rounds piling up behind the car. Another truck pulls up. It's the Big Lebowski, right down to the ratty bathrobe and scraggly beard. "Nice tree," he shouts, standing in front of me, slurping the remains of whatever's in his coffee cup – White Russian, no doubt – off his mustache. "That your wood stacked on the road?" he shouts. I shut down the saw and flip up my safety visor. "No," I say, "I was just cutting it up so you could fit it in your stove easier." He lowers his sunglasses and glares at me with bloodshot eyes for a long moment. *Uh-oh. Might have bitten off more than I can chew.* "Ha!" he says at last, slapping my shoulder with his knuckles, "Good one, bro." Then he shambles back to the truck and drives away in a cloud of diesel exhaust. The Dude abides.

That's how it is this time of year. The jet stream, recharged by our cooling northern hemisphere, drives brawling storms in from the Pacific. The storms topple trees, and you have to be prepared to drop everything and get there quick if you want to take advantage.

Anyone who lives in a house surrounded by trees has a love-hate relationship with these autumn winds. We depend on the big blows for our firewood supply, but they also mean extended power outages (power goes out on the Island whenever someone sneezes, goes the old joke) and sometimes sheer terror.

A month after Weston was born, a ferocious "100-year" storm tore through the Northwest. Our house was still under construction, so we – a newborn baby, a mother recovering from emergency C-section, a restless three-year-old girl, a crazed 20-year-old cat that howled every night, and me – were living in the small outbuilding that now serves as my office. At dusk, the wind started out of the south, like water rushing over rocks – a soft but rising white noise. In a matter of hours, the air accelerating through tree branches had taken on the ominous rumble of a waterfall. Small branches snapped and crashed against the roof. By midnight, we were engulfed in the deafening roar of a 747 powering off the runway.

Weston slept through it all, perhaps an early indication of his future talent. Skyla stirred but never fully woke. Stacy, in a haze of Percocet and postpartum hormones, tossed and turned, waking once to groggily ask, "Are we going downstream?" The old cat and I stayed up, howling through the night. At least one of us was terrified. With each big gust, I would hear the crack and pop of splintering wood nearby and hold my breath, waiting for the ground-shaking impact of massive trees crashing to earth. At first, I worried for our almost-finished new house, then the building we were in, and finally, after a particularly close call, us. I considered loading up the family and hauling ass for open ground, but it occurred to me that in most stories I'd read about people killed by falling trees, the victims were in their car. Clinging to that dubious logic, I sweated it out through the night, fear burning in my guts.

Meanwhile, in some part of my brain entirely detached from reality, there was a growing joy – giddiness even – over all the wood that would surely be mine if we could make it through the night. Of course, we survived. Trees crashed down on houses throughout the neighborhood, but thankfully nobody was hurt. And in the week that followed, I cut enough prime wood to last nearly two years. Windfall.

So I spend a good portion of every fall hoping for wind but dreading it at the same time. Last night was perfect: no property damage, no power outage, no fear. And now, this sweet madrona. I stuff my old Montero with heavy rounds until the springs bottom out, then make a quick trip to unload, worrying the whole time that someone might grab the rest of my pile while I'm gone. Two more trips and I'm done, my treasure safely stacked on pallets at the bottom of the driveway next to the big fir I scored last week. Did I mention I love madrona? If I can get to the rounds while they're still green, they'll split easily and – who knows – might even dry enough to burn by the time it gets cold winter after next. Do we have enough? I doubt it. We could use a little more wind. But not too much.

ANOTHER WORLD

My only brother's first child was born two weeks ago, on Hallow-
een. It's reason for celebration, and reason enough to pull me from
the insulated comfort of Island life into the real world: Brooklyn, New
York. Might as well be another planet. Which makes sense, since my
brother, after surviving a childhood tortured by my fish obsession –
including countless long, rainy days spent waiting in the car with our
mom while I fished – sought a different kind of life as soon as he was
able. A successful artist and fully committed New Yorker, my "little"
brother is all grown up, comfortably at home in a world I can barely
comprehend. And now he's a father. It's been a long time since we've
hung out together, and there couldn't be a better reason. I think I'm
up for it.

Tall buildings. Traffic. Sirens. Doorstep-to-doorstep pavement.
A proximity to other people's lives that my Brooklynite sister-in-law,
Sarah, finds comforting. Me? Not so much. My first night "sleeping" in a New York apartment, I learn: The kid upstairs plays basketball and his mother favors high heels; the couple next door is on the
brink of divorce; the downstairs neighbors know the words to every
song on *Cheap Trick at Budokan.* Maybe I'm too used to living in the

sticks, but I can't find any comfort in knowing when and how often the guy next door uses the bathroom.

On the other hand, urban life, especially in New York, is not without its charms. For me, that means more and better food than anywhere else on the planet. A smorgasbord of choices. I don't even know where to start. Although the purpose of this trip is to meet my baby niece and help the new parents, we still have to eat, right? I need to be careful here if I'm going to keep the gluttonous food maniac from showing through my loving-uncle-and-brother disguise.

For my first meal, I take a cab directly from the airport to Grand Sichuan in the East Village to meet my brother. He's already there when I arrive, wearing the weary, shell-shocked look of a new father. It's good to see him. He reports that baby Nora is sleeping at the moment, which takes me off the bad-uncle hook, and we're free to dive into the food. I've been dreaming of the *xiao long bao* (soup dumplings) since Adrian and I snuck out to Grand Sichuan before his wedding nearly two years ago. The dumplings do not disappoint. They arrive in a bamboo basket, trailing a fragrant, ginger-pork steam cloud. On the first bite, the tender covering melts away, releasing a broth so rich in flavor I'm almost moved to tears. As we eat, Adrian brightens and the exhaustion leaves his face. We talk more easily than we have since we were kids, sharing the new common ground of raising babies. With a little heavy-handed encouragement on my part, we also plan out every meal for the rest of my visit.

The first time I hold baby Nora in my arms, though, my one-track quest to eat everything in New York flies off the rails. She's beautiful. With my muscle memory calibrated to rambunctious 35- and 45-pounders, she feels nearly weightless and impossibly calm. It's possible that I'm biased because she's family, but I can already see great things in her small, smiling face. Either that or she really is the best baby in the world.

I imagine her coming to the Island and going fishing and crabbing and digging in the garden with us. Will she be the glamorous city girl dropping in on her barefoot hillbilly cousins? As I weigh the future possibilities, Sarah says, "Just think, your kids will be running through the water and woods while mine are running from the ranting lunatic in the subway." She said it, not me.

My New York days fall into a rhythm of holding Nora and trying to be helpful while staying out of the way of frantic new parents. When the baby sleeps, I kill time wandering around Brooklyn, window shopping and building up an appetite for my next meal. The endless stream of people is astounding. At one point, I catch my reflection in a storefront window and try to wipe the Jed Clampett look of awe off my face. In a fancy gourmet grocery store, I stumble across the very same chanterelles I was picking last week ("fresh from the Pacific Northwest") for a stunning $38 a pound. I could have paid for my trip and then some if only I'd filled my duffle bag with mushrooms instead of clothes.

In the evenings, my brother and I eat. Dinnertime is Nora's favorite nap time, and Sarah, who's juggling motherhood and graduate school, needs the peace and quiet to study. She generously offers the two food-crazed brothers a free pass between 6:00 and 9:00 p.m., and we do our best to maximize the freedom with Roman Empire–style gluttony. We stuff ourselves with a magnificent *kaiseki* service at En Brasserie, highlighted by braised pork belly in bonito broth and a satiny seafood custard; we go for a "light" dinner at Nicky's Vietnamese Sandwiches, where I can't decide between the lemongrass chicken or the pork-liver pâté *banh mi,* so I order – and polish off – both. Then, just in case we might get hungry later, we order another bagful of sandwiches to go. One night, we take a wide-awake Nora with us and "settle" for the pizza joint around the corner. I consume an entire pepperoni pizza that's better than any I've had in years.

Every day, there are Brooklyn bagels from the Bagel Hole – dense, chewy rounds with a light, crisp crust and hearty malt aroma. I eat them for breakfast and lunch – plain, with cream cheese, with the smoked king I brought from home. And once, when I've just finished off three of these heavyweight carbo-bombs, I look out the window to see – no way! – the dim sum truck? They bring dim sum *to you* here? Of course, I had to check it out, which involved *char siu baos* (steamed *and* baked), pot stickers, half a dozen *shumai* dumplings...

Through it all, my brain runs in a closed loop of two divergent thoughts: *If we had food like this at home, it would be awesome! If we had food like this at home, I would weigh 350 pounds! But if we had food like this at home, it would be awesome!* And so on.

In calmer moments, which is to say, the short periods between meals, I have some real pangs of wishing we could all live closer together, of wanting to watch Nora grow up and to be a regular part of Adrian and Sarah's life. I want our kids to feel the comfort of a life spent running around with their cousins every day, whether through water and woods or from subway lunatics. Mostly, though, I realize how much I miss my brother.

I'm also missing my own family and the soothing green forest. With every nerve-jangling siren, stranger's raised voice, or honk-ing horn, I feel like Holly Golightly's father, lost in Metropolis. (My appreciation for Buddy Ebsen's career is growing by the minute.) The massive brownstone canyons, lined with concrete and asphalt, carry a river of cars and humanity instead of water. Trees grow only from evenly spaced, well-planned gaps in the pavement. I can feel the weight of it all pressing down on me. Yet my brother navigates the urban chaos with a natural confidence; this place is home to him as much as the Island is to me. I guess it's time to give up my fantasy that he'll someday move to the Island and we'll raise our children together.

On my last day in the city, I am standing in my brother's kitch-en, rocking Nora in my arms and staring out the window. Gray November light filters through the narrow space between buildings. A squirrel runs along the fence carrying something in its mouth. It pauses to eat directly in front of the window. When I look closely, I see that it's gnawing on a chicken drumstick.

"Holy shit," I shout, frightening the sleeping baby, "there's a squirrel eating *meat!*"

"Oh," my brother says, not looking up from the baby bottle he's heating.

"That's crazy. Where I come from, squirrels eat nuts and berries...not *meat*."

Sarah glances out the window, takes the now fussing baby from my arms, and says, "That's just how we roll in Brooklyn."

Man, I'm a long way from home.

A week later, a heavy package arrives from New York. Inside I find two dozen of the densest, chewiest, finest bagels ever to exist west of the Mississippi. A gift from baby Nora. I immediately pull a bag of smoked summer king from the freezer, throw it in the microwave to thaw, and start spreading cream cheese. I heart New York.

WINTER

GOING COASTAL: GUNS AND SHOVELS

This one kicked our asses. Even worse, it was completely avoidable. As early as Tuesday, satellite pictures showed a deep low-pressure system loaded with subtropical moisture pushing across the Pacific in our direction. By Friday morning, as we packed the car, the weather service was predicting the storm would make landfall by late afternoon and continue to pound the coast for 36 hours. The marine forecast for near-shore coastal waters: *South wind 25 to 35 knots, gusting to 50. Wind waves 7 to 9 feet. West swell 24 feet at 11 seconds. Rain heavy at times.* We were heading right into the teeth of it. But at least we'd be on a completely exposed beach. In the surf. At night.

We should have known better. But we were *committed:* cabin rented, gear packed, friends on the way to meet us. The kids were excited; the parents were excited; we were all ready to go. And this was about more than just razor clams. We had tradition to uphold and we weren't going to bag it on account of a weather forecast. (Okay, actually, I wanted to bag it, but the optimists in the family prevailed.)

For the past 10 years, Stacy and our friend Candace have celebrated their birthdays (which fall within a week of each other) with a gathering of friends on the coast. While the stated purpose is digging razor clams, delectable bivalves that thrive on wave-battered ocean beaches, these trips are as much about time with friends as they are about seafood. Each year, as autumn dissolves into winter, we rent a cabin near the beach and spend long hours digging in the surf and late nights gathered around a propane stove, cleaning clams.

We still talk about the gorgeous shirtsleeve November evening when we stopped digging to watch a crimson sun melt into the flat-calm Pacific. Or the time Jennifer's fleece jacket caught on fire and we all stood around in shock until Sweeney saved the day by rolling her on the ground to extinguish the flames. Or the late tide when everyone dropped their limits on the porch and went to bed, leaving Glen, Sweeney, and me to clean clams until it was nearly light out again. My favorite memory, though, is of Stacy, nine months pregnant with Weston, digging a limit of razors even though she could barely kneel to reach them. Five days later, she went into labor.

Friday afternoon. Not a drop of rain has fallen on the three-hour drive to the coast, and Weston and Skyla combined have only asked "Are we there yet?" nine times. (Note: To combat this exasperating question, I've taken to simply answering, "Yes," regardless of our location.) We have made only three bathroom stops. All good. The wind, though, is picking up. Alder saplings along the highway flail in the breeze, and a hail of old leaves, fir needles, and small twigs bounces off the windshield. But it's dry. "Maybe it won't be so bad," Stacy says. "It's not even raining."

Candace and Glen are running late, and the Sweeneys had to wait for Maren to get out of school, so we'll be digging on our own, at least to start. After unloading a year's supply of clothing and groceries into the weekend rental cabin, we armor up in rubber boots, fleece, and full rain gear. Weston clambers around the cabin with a stiff-limbed, Tin Man gait, while I sort out the lanterns and hurry us along. "Come on, you guys, we gotta go," I yell. "It's going to be dark soon."

That's one of the things about winter razor-clam digs. They are scheduled around minus tides, which at this time of year happen at night. If it's an early enough tide (tonight, the low of –1.7 feet is at 7:30 p.m.) and conditions are good, you can usually dig your limit of clams before dark. And *everything* is easier before dark: finding clams, digging them up, getting back to your car, and – especially important with small children – keeping track of everyone.

We drive to the beach and from the top of the dunes look down at an ominous river of sand flowing north. A waist-high layer of wind-borne grit courses up the beach, twisting, turning, streaming around obstructions and reconnecting below them like water moving downhill. Across this hellish Saharan scene, a huge ocean swell running ahead of the storm pounds into the beach and surges upward. Wind tears the top off each wave and swirls a mist of salt spray into the flying sand. When I open the car door, it's jerked out of my hand and nearly blown off its hinges.

I'm somehow comforted by the fact that we are not the only idiots out here today. A steady stream of trucks is pouring onto the beach, and the line of parked cars extends as far as we can see in either direction. With razor clam "openers" limited to a few weekends a year, it isn't uncommon for 15,000 diggers to converge for a single tide. Since some clam diggers are either smarter than we are or not as tough (I prefer the latter explanation), the crowd will be a little thinner tonight. We won't get lonely, though. On the lee side of each truck, people are getting ready, strapping mesh clam bags on wader belts, struggling to light lanterns in the wind, yelling to be heard over booming surf and the hiss of flying sand.

It's a strange scene. Down along the surf line, hundreds of people have gathered. Many of them are walking backward, tapping the sand with weirdly shaped shovels or long metal tubes. Under ideal conditions – falling tide, calm surf, no wind – buried razor clams mark their location with a "show," a small dimple created when they retract their siphons. In heavy weather, though, the clams are either reluctant to extend their siphons or the "shows" get scrubbed away by surging water and wind. On a day like today, they're tough to find.

The only hope is to force the clams to suddenly withdraw their siphons, leaving a short-lived "show" that can be spotted by a practiced eye. Stomping feet and pounding shovels are the preferred way to make this happen. If you beamed down from another planet – Brooklyn, New York, say – and saw 10,000 people walking backward in circles, hitting the ground with shovels and squinting through the gloom, you might assume you had stumbled into some primitive religious ritual, or gathering mass hysteria. Even if you're participating, when you look up from your stomping and squinting to watch the masses around you doing the same, it's easy to question your sanity.

Crowds are not a problem. There are no secrets to protect on a razor-clam dig. Everyone joins in the fun, and a friendly, collegial atmosphere surrounds the proceedings. At least, under normal conditions. Today, with the flying sand and surf, the mood leans more to the grim side. But we're here, so we might as well get to it. If we're lucky, we can dig a limit (15 clams per person) or two and be off the beach before we need lanterns.

We lean into the wind and trudge down to the water, where the churning waves run up onto the beach in broad sheets. (Note: Before anyone calls Child Protective Services with an endangerment complaint, I'd like to point out that the beach here has such a low gradient that the waves are only inches deep when they reach the digging zone.) Blobs of brown bubbles – wind foam – roll across the beach like tumbleweeds. The wall of flying sand, waist-high to me, hits Weston and Skyla right in the chops. When I kneel to ask if they want to go back to the cabin, I get an instant facial exfoliation and feel grit crunching between my teeth. "No," Skyla shouts, "I want to dig clams!" Weston spreads his arms and backs into the wind. "I'm flying!" he yells.

So we stomp our feet and tap the ground. "There's one!" Skyla says, pointing to a pea-sized dimple that appears next to my bootprint. "It's probably too small," I say. Because razor clams are fragile and generally don't survive the digging process, the law requires you to keep the first fifteen clams you dig, regardless of size. The big boys, their brown, rectangular shells stretching to six inches, are the ones you want. Most of the time, they make a "show" about the size of a quarter. "If we're going to get our clams, we better get 'em now," Stacy says. And with that, she puts the business end of her clam "gun" into the sand around the small show and drives it in.

A clam gun is a simple but ingenious tool: Two feet of four-inch-diameter metal tubing necked down to a hollow one-inch crossbar handle on top. The open bottom end of the wide tube is placed where you believe the clam to be and pushed into the sand. There's a small hole on the handle that you cover with a thumb to create suction when you extract the tube. The tube comes free with a four-inch-wide cylinder of sand – and, ideally, the razor clam – inside. Releasing your thumb breaks the vacuum, depositing the sand cylinder and clam on the beach. This is Stacy's weapon of choice, and her baby-blue aluminum clam gun has proven deadly over the years, especially when water runs over the beach the way it is tonight.

She drops the sand cylinder and the kids dive on it, pawing through the packed grit, but it's empty. No clam. They must be deep today. I reach into the hole with my hand, scooping the collapsing sand out. When I'm in over my elbow, I feel the sharp edges of a shell – they don't call them *razors* for nothing – and carefully grip the sides and wiggle until it comes loose. "Weston," I say, "reach down in there and see if you can find the clam...I can't reach it." He eagerly shoulders me aside, lies flat on his stomach in liquid sand, and plunges his arm in. He frowns in concentration while his fingers sift through the muck. Then his eyes open wide and he shouts, "I got it! I got a clam!" At five inches long, it's hardly the peanut I was expecting.

After considerable searching, I find a good show behind a receding wave, drop to my knees and start digging. In spite of Stacy's success with the gun, I've stuck with the same old-school clam shovel

I've used since I was a kid. It has a four-foot wooden handle and nar-row, curving blade with a blunt, squared-off tip. Razor clams tend to burrow slightly toward the water from their show, so you dig from the land side, using the angled blade to lever chunks of sand away from your clam. But you don't dig all the way; any contact with the shovel would crush a razor clam's thin shell. So you take a few scoops and finish the operation with your hand. At least, that's how it's sup-posed to work.

This time, just as I set the shovel aside and reach in for the clam, another wave surges up the beach, caving in the hole and soaking me to the core. To avoid further drenching, I abandon the clam and stand up, just in time to catch a gust of wind-driven grit and salt spray in the face. My hat blows off and tumbles into the water, skip-ping along just out of reach. Awesome.

Tonight, we're going to have to work as a team. The four of us walk backward into the wind in crescent formation, me pounding with the shovel handle and the kids, closer to the ground, looking for shows. When they spot one, Stacy moves in with the gun. It's a good rhythm, and the next 10 clams come in quick succession. We exchange wet, sandy high-fives, laughing and joking, oblivious to the weather, fully engrossed in our little four-person world.

And then, we aren't finding clams anymore. I stomp harder, the kids crouch lower to examine the sand for any trace of life, and... nothing. "Dad," Skyla says, "We can't see any shows now." I look up to an eerie, beautiful sight: Thousands of glowing lanterns moving back and forth along the waterline, defining the curve of the beach for miles to the north. No wonder we can't see any clams. It's get-ting dark.

"Okay," I say, "wait right here with Mom, and stay out of the water." I jog up to where I think the car should be (only it's not), and knowing we've been working our way south, start walking up the line of parked cars. The wind velocity has picked up, and now the rain starts, pelting my jacket and hood like shotgun pellets. I finally find the car, much farther north than I expected, and try to light the lantern. Easier said than done. With the wind and wet hands it takes approximately 45 matches. The bright, cheerful glow comes as a relief.

As I'm locking up, Candace, Glen, and the Sweeneys pull in and pile out. "Nice weather," someone shouts. By now, Stacy and the kids have been on the beach in the dark for half an hour, so I say a quick hello and hustle back down the beach. Halfway there, a monstrous gust knocks me sideways and blows out the lantern. It takes another 45 matches to get it lit again.

When I reach them, Stacy and Skyla have somehow located a clam in the dark and are gunning it up. Weston sits next to them in a shallow depression, waist-deep in water. He looks up at me with a guilty smile. Skyla's raincoat flaps in the wind and her teeth chatter. "Let's go in," Stacy says. "I think we've had enough." "But Dad just got back with the lantern," Skyla says through quivering lips. "Let's dig five more clams." We settle on two, dig them, and call it a night.

We stumble back to the car and find the Sweeneys already there. With eight clams in their bag, they're packing it in, too. We gather around the back of their Suburban, peeling wet, gritty gear off shivering kids. In a stroke of genius, Sweeney has brought a barrel-sized beverage cooler filled with hot water. When he opens the spigot, we rinse our hands, and Weston's whole body, under the steaming flow. "Maybe tomorrow it'll be better," Stacy says. "It has to let up sometime, right?"

Long after the kids have warmed up in hot baths, filled their bellies with cheesy noodles in front of the fire, and nestled into sleeping bags, Candace and Glen show up dripping wet, wind-blasted, and limited out. "Thirty clams the hard way," Glen says. Stacy pulls birthday lasagnas from the oven – one made with multicolored Northern Lights chard and a creamy béchamel sauce, the other bubbling with red sauce made from the last of our windowsill-ripened tomatoes. In our haste to consume maximum warm calories, we forget to sing "Happy Birthday," but nobody seems to mind. Glasses of malbec are raised, more lasagna eaten, and just as I'm drifting into a happy, hazy dream world, Mia starts the coffee. There's still work to do.

Like most shellfish, razor clams need to be cleaned while they're still alive to prevent bacterial growth. And that means now, regardless of fatigue, overeating, or any of a hundred other good reasons to lie on the couch and doze. Thankfully, the cabin has a garage, so we'll be working out of the weather.

Glen fires up the propane stove, and in memory of the Great Fleece Jacket Fire, we give it a wide berth as we bustle around in our combustible synthetic insulation. Our old black-enameled Dutch oven, half filled with fresh water, goes onto the stove, and when it comes to a boil, I dip a mesh bag of clams into the pot just long enough for the shells to pop open. Then it's a quick rinse in a bucket of ice water to keep them from cooking, and they're good to go. Let the cleaning begin.

The clams slide easily out of their shells, and with a pair of old scissors we snip the tough siphon tips off and cut along one side from top to bottom until each body opens up like a butterfly. Digestive organs are sliced away, and the foot, or digger, is separated from the body and filleted to remove the organs inside. What remains of each clam are two succulent pieces of meat: the flat, oblong disk of body and siphon, with a big hole in the middle where the guts used to be, and the tender, boot-shaped foot. From a good clam, the doughnut-shaped main body "steak" will more than cover your hand, and the foot will be a third that size. With small "peanut" razors, the edible parts are minuscule. The amount of work, though, is the same, and the importance of targeting bigger clams becomes readily apparent after a few minutes over the cleaning bucket.

It's two o'clock in the morning when we rinse the last bits of sand from our cleaned clams and sort them into ziplocks. There's nothing like standing on a cold concrete slab in the middle of the night to take the starch out of you. Every joint in my body seems to have fused, but we're done. Hallelujah. But wait. "The clam guts are going to bring in raccoons, don't you think?" Sweeney asks. We pull on our boots and wet, sandy rain gear and haul the gutbuckets down to the beach in a raging typhoon. "This is insane," Glen says. "It's gotta let up sometime, right?"

Saturday morning. After a long night of restless sleep, with wind howling outside the cabin and rain rattling and gurgling through downspouts, we've got 12 hours to kill before the evening dig. Nobody wants to spend the day trapped inside a small cabin with four wild banshee children, either.

So we drive north to fish a small estuary known for its big coastal silver salmon. It's running chocolate brown with storm runoff today, and the locals tossing lures into the dark current look glum. Sweeney and I make a few halfhearted casts and give up when a full-size refrigerator comes floating downstream along with what looks like half of a house. We hike up into the forest searching for chanterelles, but heavy, soaking brush and the occasional falling fir tree drive us back to the car within minutes. We take the kids down to the jetty to watch the storm pounding ashore, but find towering green waves exploding over the rocks and flooding the parking lot.

Trapped in a small cabin with four wild banshee children it is.

The afternoon passes slowly, but the kids, much to everyone's surprise, remain calm. After our brief foray into the deluge, they're perfectly content to enjoy the coziness of warm shelter. Weston talks Sweeney (then Glen, then me) into "dinosaur wrestling" on the carpeted floor, and when he's worn us all out settles for watching football on TV. Skyla alternates between drawing and sounding out words in her reading-lesson book. The older girls, Laine and Maren, play a board game, then help Glen make corn tortillas for tonight's dinner.

I'm having a hard time settling in. This forced captivity takes some serious recalibration. Without my never-ending list of home projects to work on, I am forced to relax. After pacing back and forth for a while, staring at the weather through rain-spattered windows, I eventually sit back on the couch and watch the Huskies lose another football game. I can't remember the last time I lounged around doing nothing during daylight hours. It's a little disorienting. But I think I could get used to it.

Meanwhile, the storm keeps pummeling the beach and rocking the cabin to its foundation.

Glen is making deer tacos for dinner, stewing down an enormous pot of ground venison, whole-roasted peppers, onions, and tomatoes with plenty of garlic and cumin. The kids scoop balls of wet masa into a press, pushing down on the lever and dropping tortillas onto a griddle. Mia sets out a big fillet of smoked salmon and crackers. Stacy opens a jar of our garden salsa and an industrial-size bag of chips. I contribute by intermittently prying myself off the couch to hover around the kitchen and sample the food.

When we all sit down to dinner – a somewhat pointless formality since we've been eating continuously for the past five hours – the long parade of trucks starts rumbling past the cabin, headed for the beach. Tonight, though, there's an equally long procession of trucks turning around and heading back in the other direction. Even the tough-as-nails Olympic Peninsula locals are retreating. Full of good food, warm and comfortable, I can't imagine going back out into the storm. Clamming hasn't even crossed my mind. Glen pushes back from the table, looks out into the dusk, and says, "We're here. I'm going." Bastard.

We're all going. We march into the ferocious wind, leaning forward at a 45-degree angle to the ground, hoods cinched tight and still flapping around our faces. Bigger gusts push the kids sideways and the glow sticks I hung around their necks fly out behind them. My glasses are streaked with rain and sand, leaving me looking through a kaleidoscope of lantern glare at vague shapes of light and dark. To quote my brother, "Does the fun ever start?"

I would like to say that our heroic effort is rewarded with a bounty of razor clams. Or even a few. But 40 minutes into it, when a particularly substantial blast of wind blows our last working lantern out, we surrender and head back to the cabin, tails between our legs. In our combined clam bags (seven of us were optimistic enough to carry one) resides a single, lonely razor clam that was spotted by Laine and gunned by Stacy. It is approximately 1½ inches long. "Well," Stacy says, "at least we won't be up late cleaning clams tonight."

Sunday night. Now that we're home, my enthusiasm has returned with the anticipation of dinner. This morning, with the season closed and no way for us to legally dig, Mother Nature got the last laugh: The day dawned bright blue, unseasonably warm, and without a hint of wind. It had to let up sometime, right? We drove home under a pearly blue sky, and when we stopped for lunch, Skyla and Weston changed into shorts and flip-flops.

It's time to start cooking. When you order "fried clams" at most any restaurant these days, you'll likely get a basket of previously frozen, dough-covered pebbles of vaguely clam-flavored mystery meat. These bear about as much resemblance to a home-cooked razor clam as Vienna sausages do to a prime, aged porterhouse. Which is to say, razor clams are something special.

I rinse the clams again with great care – a single, crunching grain of sand can ruin it for me – and place them on paper towels to drain. Using a heavy wooden meat-tenderizing hammer that Bob Dawson made for me, I give each siphon section, the chewiest part of the clam, a few shots to soften it up. Weston asks to take over the hammering procedure, but thinking of our countertop, his fingers, and my fingers, none of which would benefit from tenderizing, I redirect him to scrambling eggs for the breading.

Once the clams have been pounded, our preparation is the same as for oysters: I lightly season the clams with garlic salt and Lawry's, roll them in a flour-cornmeal mix, give them a quick dip in Weston's beaten eggs, and finish with panko. Then I drop them into a heavy pan filled with a third of an inch of peanut oil and flip them when the bottom side turns golden brown. A light sprinkle of kosher salt when they come out of the pan, and it's almost impossible to wait until the clams cool to eat them. I invariably burn my tongue "making sure they're okay" before serving the family.

This time, though, I'm going to be patient. While I wait for the first batch to cool, I look around at the vast collection of soaked and sand-covered waders, jackets, boots, and hats hanging near the woodstove. I remember thinking last night, at the moment our final lantern blew out, *nobody's stupid enough to be out here in this.* I remind myself to pay attention to the weather next time, learn something, be smarter.

Stacy and the kids come into the kitchen and we gather around the rack of cooling clams for a family sampling. With the second batch, we will sit down to our real dinner, but these first ones, well, who can wait for plates and utensils? We'll eat with our hands, standing in the kitchen. Weston and Skyla each grab a tender foot piece (their preferred part) and reach for another before they're done with the first. Stacy sinks her teeth into one of the big bodies and closes her eyes. I crunch into my first bite of crisp crust and sweet, clean ocean flavor. We should have known better. But I'm glad we didn't.

PRIUS ENVY

Outside the local organic food store, it takes me three tries to squeeze my old Montero into the tiny parking space. I am wedged between a biodiesel Volkswagen and a shiny new Prius. I open my door slowly to avoid dinging the glossy Toyota paint, crane my neck, and slide carefully out. At this moment, a stylish fleece-and–Gore-Tex–clad woman exits the store with two bags of groceries, walks to the Prius, and pauses before getting in. I catch her eye, expecting a thank-you for being so careful, or at least a nod. But no. She looks at me, looks at my 19-year-old SUV, then wrinkles her nose and shakes her head in withering disapproval.

Perhaps during the manic days of summer fishing, or the hurly-burly autumn harvest, I wouldn't even notice such things. But it's 38 degrees outside, a light, misty rain has been falling since I can't remember when, and at 4:17 in the afternoon, it's already dark. Winter. A time when small incidents like this take root in your brain, and the long nights provide ample hours in which to turn them around and examine them from different angles. If you're not careful, you can ruminate yourself right into insomnia.

I want to do the right thing. I really do. As a fisherman, forager, and father of two young children, of course I want to do what's right.

I would like to drive a hybrid, live in a house built from recycled materials, eat only organic, sustainable food, and act as a responsible steward for our planet. But as I am finding, unless you have pretty deep pockets and plenty of time on your hands, that's a lot easier said than done. It's even tougher to accept that "doing what's right," might require some real sacrifice, especially where recreation is concerned. So, like many who aspire to do better by Mother Earth, when faced with the everyday realities of life, I rationalize. It's the only way to get a good night's sleep.

Take my car, for example. It might be old and beat up (I recently had to pull weeds growing out of the window sills), but it's perfect for hauling kids, camping equipment, clam gear, and crab pots, and the high ground clearance and four-wheel drive make it possible to launch our boat on steep ramps and soft beaches. It's no F250 when it comes to moving large quantities of firewood, but if I take out the kid seats and stuff it to the ceiling, I can make do. It gets about 18 miles per gallon – not bad for a mid size SUV – but apparently that's not enough to ward off dirty looks in the parking lot.

Hell yeah, I'd like to drive a shiny new Prius. Ideally, I'd have one for grocery shopping (especially at the organic food store), taking the kids to soccer, and other gear-free errands. Of course, I'd still need an SUV for everything else. And while we're at it, why not throw in that F250 for hauling wood? Trouble is, I spend so much time fishing and chasing the kids around, I really don't have the financial wherewithal to be a two-car guy, let alone a three. Thus, the beater Montero.

So here comes my rationalization: Since I work from home and don't commute, if I traded in my car for something more fuel efficient, it's a pretty sure bet the SUV's new owner would drive it more than I do. In other words, the old Montero would still be on the road burning more gas than it does now. Even if I could afford to just scrap it, there are issues of landfill and waste to consider.

And what about the new car? It takes significant amounts of energy, raw materials, and transportation to build a Prius – or any new car, for that matter. If I bought one, I'd be on the hook for the new car's manufacturing footprint and fuel use as well as the emissions from someone else driving my old car. So...by keeping the Montero and driving it as little as possible, I'm really doing what's best for the earth. At least that's what I tell myself so I can sleep at night.

Then there's the house. Several years ago, with Weston on the way and our living situation already cramped, Stacy and I decided to build a pretty significant addition to our old home in the woods. Spurred on by a growing awareness of human impact on the environment – not to mention the ubiquitous "sustainable building" media buzz – we started with all kinds of idealistic thoughts on how to make it an earth-friendly project.

Turns out, being green on a budget is an uphill battle only Sisyphus could fully appreciate. Recycled wood products? Be prepared to pay through the teeth, as the cost of labor to strip, clean, and re-mill old lumber far outweighs what it takes to simply chop down trees. What about reusing existing windows and flooring? Again, it's far cheaper to dump the old and start from scratch with factory-fresh stuff. New windows are also much more energy efficient, but do you gain enough to make up for the manufacturing and transportation? The mind reels. How about a tankless, on-demand hot water heater? Get ready to hear "they don't work for crap" from a lot of plumbers. It goes on and on. You push the "green" boulder up the hill and the force of reality rolls it right back down.

I don't blame those who work in the trades. They'd rather do what they've always done because they need to count on the results. With their names and bank accounts on the line, few can afford to experiment. So unless you find a contractor who specializes in sustainable building, it's going to be tough. And if you do, there's a good chance it's going to be expensive.

Still, we did find a little good news. Sustainable bamboo flooring is tough, beautiful, and relatively affordable. It might not be recycled, but at least you aren't cutting down slow-growing hardwoods or old-growth fir to walk on. Of course, I don't know how shipping bamboo from Asia and, even worse, trucking it from the port of entry to my home factor into the whole equation, but examining every possible angle is a sure recipe for sleeplessness.

That hot water heater? After dozens of calls and meetings with five different plumbers, we finally found a guy who was in love with the Rinnai tankless water heaters from Japan. He told us that the negative reports about this kind of appliance (lack of reliability and insufficient power to heat our cold Northwest groundwater) were based on other, better-known brands. He would sell, install, and stand behind the Rinnai without reservation. It cost about twice what you'd pay for a traditional water heater, which keeps 50 gallons of water hot even when you're not using it. In theory, by heating only what we needed, when we needed it, the Rinnai would save us enough in energy costs to pay the difference within two years. Remarkably, it has.

A little less obvious – and a whole lot less sexy – are the benefits we found in manufactured-wood floor joists. Instead of solid beams cut from large old fir trees, these are made from small pieces of wood, sawdust, and other waste (think of them as tree sausages) compressed under tons of weight to form incredibly strong, straight timbers. In fact, they're so straight, installation is a snap, reducing labor costs to make up for the higher purchase price. Sure, there are questions about the energy, and in some cases the formaldehyde-based glue used in manufacturing, but too many details tend to get in the way of a good rationalization.

I spent countless hours pulling nails from old flooring and siding that was removed during the demolition process. Our contractor used this salvaged wood wherever possible to lower material costs and reduce the number of trees that went into the project. But the math here only worked because I employed free, unskilled labor (me) to sit on the porch with a hammer, pry bar, lantern, and plenty of late-night talk radio. The virgin lumber we did use came from a Canadian company known for sustainable forest management, and I will say we paid dearly for it. But I guess that's a predictable result of trying to manage a construction project without professional help: After doing the research, I was so excited about this company's timber practices, I placed the order without asking what the bill was going to be; when it came, I almost passed out. A friend called it "further evidence of another failed financial strategy."

So, did we build a "green" house? Not even close. No hay-bale or recycled-concrete walls. No reclaimed oak floors. No salvaged slate roofing or refurbished doors. The fact is, most of the really cool stuff we simply couldn't afford. But we did the best we could, given our available time and money. Or at least that's what I tell myself so I can sleep at night.

As long as I'm going to be tossing and turning on this winter night, I might as well dive in all the way and take a look at the cost of our recreation. In what might be the outdoor enthusiast's ultimate irony, the process of loving and experiencing nature is, to varying degrees, destroying it. More specifically, the act of getting to and from "nature" causes a lot of the harm. Trucks, motorboats, long drives, paved roads...they all damage the very thing we're traveling to experience. The all-or-none runoff pattern from impermeable asphalt creates sudden flooding and longer periods of drought in our river systems. Beyond the obvious effects of exhaust on the atmosphere, our cars leak oil, transmission fluid, and poisonous metal brake dust that all eventually end up in the water. You could always move out to the country and live where you recreate (which is, to some extent, what we are trying to do on the Island), but then you'd probably have a long commute to wherever you worked. And living in the boonies means more everyday driving to schools, grocery stores, soccer practice, etc. All this, done by people who actually care very deeply about the outdoors.

What about the vast majority of people and corporations for whom the natural world is at best an insignificant diversion and at worst a detriment to their bottom lines?

When BP says there's nothing to worry about, that they have triple redundancy on a mechanical "blowout protector" submerged beneath thousands of feet of corrosive saltwater, I worry. When Aquabounty tells us their new genetically engineered food product (a fast-growing Atlantic salmon with growth hormone genes from Chinook salmon and a genetic "on switch" from the ocean pout fish) is "identical in every measurable way to the traditional food Atlantic salmon," I worry. When Northern Dynasty assures us that their enormous open-pit, cyanide-leach mine, planned for the headwaters of Bristol Bay, won't damage the world's last great wild salmon rivers, I worry.

Where does that leave those of us who depend on the outdoors for our day-to-day mental health? I can only hope that somehow, through participating in the natural world, our need to protect it becomes more urgent. Maybe understanding what we have, what we've lost, and what we stand to lose can spur us to action. Maybe it will force us to stand up and fight the BPs, Aquabounties and Northern Dynasties of the world. Whether or not that action can actually save what we love has yet to be seen, but I do know this: We have to try, if for no other reason than to get a good night's sleep.

I want to do the right thing. I really do. I want Skyla and Weston to live in a world that's at least as rich as the one we have now, if not better. But I'm full of hypocrisy, rationalization, and conflict. I admit it. It's been pointed out that if I truly wanted to do what's best for the environment, I would live in an energy-efficient high-rise condominium, in a densely populated urban area where I could walk everywhere I needed to go. I would not water a yard. I would not burn wood for heat. And I certainly would not drive anywhere to fish or forage. I would have very little impact on the natural world. Of course, I'd never experience it, either. But it would be out there, all the healthier for my absence.

I wonder how the lady with the Prius sleeps at night? Probably better than I do. At the organic food store checkout counter, a kid with blond dreadlocks bulging from a Bob Marley knit cap informs me (a little more emphatically than I think necessary) that they most certainly do *not* carry Lunesta. He suggests melatonin instead. Great. Give me the biggest jar you have. I think I'm going to need it.

THE SIGNIFICANCE OF BIRDS IV

"Dad," Skyla says in a dramatic whisper, "there's an eagle *right* there!" Weston and I follow her pointing finger to an alder branch 15 feet directly above us. I catch my breath. Up close, an adult bald eagle is an immense bird. It cocks its head and stares down at us, but makes no move to fly away.

A few minutes later, Weston hooks a small trout and hauls it to the bank. I reach down to unhook it and glance back to make sure the eagle is still there. Then I toss the struggling trout out into the pond, and as it leaves my hand, the eagle lifts off, wheels around and drops with extended talons. We can hear air swishing through feathers and water shearing when it plucks the trout from the surface and returns to its perch. The kids and I look at each other with wide eyes.

There was an osprey out over the water, stark white against a pale winter sky, its slender wings barely moving as it hovered on the breeze. From time to time, it would make a halfhearted dive before aborting the mission and flapping back to altitude. I stared at the osprey, hoping with all the concentration a 10–year-old boy could muster that I might will it to succeed.

We were fishing. Or we were going fishing, although I can't recall making a cast or catching any fish that day. What I remember is the osprey, and my dad saying that when we moved back to Oregon in the spring, he wouldn't be going with us.

After that, neither of us spoke for a long time. My mind raced with questions, but I was too afraid of the answers to ask. Maybe we kept fishing. The osprey was still there, farther away now, a distant speck hunting back and forth across open water. Suddenly, it folded its wings and dropped from the sky, accelerating toward something I couldn't see.

ON THE ROAD

Driving to our house, you leave the paved access road down by the mailboxes and turn onto a narrow gravel lane bordered by salmonberries on one side and an enormous, thorny wall of Himalaya blackberries on the other. A hundred yards deeper into the woods, an even narrower dirt two-track takes you down the hill to our house. When you start seeing blue tarps, buckets, and freight pallets, you're getting close.

It's that first section of gravel road we share with four neighbors that concerns me, especially during the rainy season. (Which, this year, feels about 11 months long.) When the first autumn storms come, the road's solid, sunbaked surface holds up fine. For a while. Then, after months of steady winter precipitation, the ground saturates and standing water appears in even the shallowest depressions.

And that means potholes. If you don't get on it, the holes grow at an exponential rate, going from a little bouncy to suspension-wrecking in a matter of days.

It's a vicious cycle. Water collects in a shallow puddle, someone drives through it, and a few rocks splash out. More water collects and the next car splashes more rocks out, allowing even more water to collect, etc, etc. Water is the enemy. And if it keeps raining, you end up with holes big enough to swallow a Volkswagen.

A couple of years ago, over on the Olympic Peninsula (where nearly 12 feet of rain falls each year), I drove down an old gravel road into a pothole so deep, the boat I was towing floated its trailer off the ground. Water came pouring into my car through the door seals, flooding the floorboard; if it had been any deeper, it would have killed the motor. My passenger, an Olympic Peninsula local, said, "Oh, good. I was worried the road might be in bad shape." He wasn't being sarcastic, either.

You just have to stay on top of things. If you patch the road at the first sign of standing water, it only takes a little gravel and hardly any effort at all. Wait too long, though, and fixing the road becomes a big, unpleasant job requiring heavy loads of rock and serious labor. The lesson is obvious: Procrastination hurts.

So, of course, I put off patching the road through two solid weeks of rain and watched with gnawing concern as the potholes grew larger each day. I knew I should fix them, but more urgent (or enjoyable) projects kept getting in the way. By the time the situation became dire enough to make it my top priority, the holes were so big that the job seemed too daunting. So I put it off for another few days. And now, as they say, it's time to pay the piper.

Maybe you're wondering why one of the other four families doesn't fix the road. Good question. And there's a simple answer: Five years ago, the neighbors decided they'd had it with muddy cars, abused suspensions, and the dangers of careening around the road trying to avoid holes. They voted to pave the road with smooth, permanent, maintenance-free asphalt. But one of the neighbors – clearly in the minority – talked them out of it, citing runoff issues and other environmental concerns, finishing up with a vigorous pooh-poohing of the work needed to maintain a gravel road. That genius was me. And now I feel responsible for the whole thing.

At least today I have my right-hand man on the job. Weston recently celebrated his fourth birthday and, as an official "big boy," has proclaimed himself ready to help with the roadwork. We take two shovels (a grown-up model and a small plastic beach toy designed for sand castle construction) and a five-gallon bucket up the road to the pile of crushed rock sitting in our neighbor's front yard. Compared to my early days on the one-man road crew, the simple existence of this reserve gravel makes the job drastically easier.

When I first took over responsibility for the road, patching it required a trip (or several, depending on how long I'd procrastinated) to the lumberyard to load up on 80-pound bags of gravel. I'd pile them into the back of my car until the springs bottomed out, then drive down our road throwing bags out next to potholes. It was expensive, time consuming, and let me just say not exactly a picnic moving the bags of rock around.

Every time I had to wrestle one of those miserable hernia-traps into position, I thought of John Huelsdonk, the legendary Olympic Peninsula pioneer known as the Iron Man of the Hoh. As the first, and hardiest, of the settlers who tried to scratch out a living on the Hoh River in the 1890s, he was renowned for his great strength (hence the nickname) and determination. As the story goes, a ranger came across Huelsdonk climbing a steep grade with a cast-iron woodstove strapped to his back, and was moved to comment on the difficult task. In response, Huelsdonk reportedly said that the stove wasn't a problem, it was the 50-pound sack of flour flopping around inside that made it tough.

Now we have it easy. Every few years, when the road reaches the point where maintenance becomes a full-time job, we call in the professionals. They bring heavy equipment to regrade the roadbed, making sure there's enough camber (side-to-side tilt) to keep water from pooling. Truckloads of new gravel are brought in and rolled and tamped into place. I finally got smart enough to have the road crew deliver a few extra yards of gravel and leave it in a heap for easy access. The last time they came, we went with recycled, crushed concrete instead of our usual quarried black basalt, relying on reports that it holds up better and keeps old sidewalks and foundations out of landfills. It also has the right ratio of "fines" (small particles of rock and sand) to rocks for a smooth, durable surface. But it's hardly maintenance-free.

Weston scrambles to the top of the crushed concrete heap and tries to push his shovel into it. After a year of exposure to weather, the fines have done their job well, solidifying enough to repel the flimsy beach toy. He watches me driving the metal shovel in and filling the bucket. "Dad," he says, "I...need the *real* shovel." Without thinking, I hand it to him, and before I can issue my standard "Be careful," he swings it wildly toward the gravel mound. The blade misses my nose by an inch, clangs off the rocks and bounces out of his hands.

"Weston!"

"What?"

"Give me the goddam – I mean, hey...why don't we do the shoveling together?"

I grip the shovel handle in front of his hands and Weston "helps" me scoop gravel into the bucket. When it's full, I lift the bucket and start staggering up the road toward the potholes. Weston runs to help and grabs the side of the bucket, forcing us both into an awkward sideways crabwalk. Right as I'm about to bark at him to let go, I look down and see him smiling at me. "Fixing the road with you is fun," he says. We haul it the rest of the way together. For the record, 100 yards is a long way to walk sideways carrying a 40-pound bucket of rocks with a four-year-old hanging off the handle.

There's still some standing water at the bottom of the bigger holes. You don't want to dump gravel into water, as it separates the rocks from the fines and won't hold. The pros use a leaf blower to spray the water out, but I don't have one. I do, however, have Weston. Using a combination of hands, plastic shovel and lots of jumping and splashing, he manages to do the leaf blower's work in short order. He's covered in mud and soaking wet, but I don't expect anything less from him.

When he finishes clearing the first hole, I use the "real" shovel to break up the hard edges so the new rock can mesh better with the old. Our hard-won bucket of rock fills about a third of the hole, making this at minimum a 15-gallon pothole. To increase efficiency, I tell Weston to start dewatering the next hole while I go back for another bucket. I make the solo round trip in half the time as before, but find it's less than one tenth the fun.

We fill the hole to just above the surrounding road surface, and Weston brings another specialized skill to the operation. "Jump up and down real hard right here," I say, and he's more than happy to comply. It's surprising how much force a 35-pound bundle of energy can exert. Within minutes, the slight mound is packed down to level. I feather out the edges to make sure our patch won't trap more water, and our pothole is gone. One down, eight to go.

The rest of our afternoon proceeds accordingly although, with individual tasks now defined, we work a little faster and with better results. Despite my stiffening back and sore hands, I have to admit that I'm having fun. All the times I've done this job by myself over the years, the work has been easier and more efficient. But I don't recall it ever being fun.

Finally, we look up at what was, just a few hours (and blisters) ago, a cratered surface, and feel the satisfaction of seeing only level road. It won't last. Just until the next rain. Right now, though, it's as smooth as the interstate and, in a funny way, beautiful. Weston tears off toward the house, skids to a stop, and looks up into the sky. "Dad," he shouts back to me, "I just felt a drop. It's raining... Yaaaaaay!"

DEEP FREEZE

A week after Thanksgiving, winter locks us in a vise-grip of arctic cold. Brittle, frozen air normally kept at bay by our seasonal monsoon pushes south out of British Columbia and settles in for the foreseeable future. The spongy, muddy ground crunches underfoot at first, then solidifies, bringing an abrupt end to chanterelle season. The alders and maples around the house stand motionless, bare and skeletal against metallic blue skies.

I know this is standard fare for a lot of the country, but for us maritime Northwesterners, it's a brutal shock to the system. Our houses don't handle it much better. There's a run on pipe fittings and shop vacs at the hardware store, and plumbing trucks fly around the Island from one ice-geyser emergency to another. Give us 45 degrees with endless rain and we can manage. Put us in the freezer, and suddenly our clothes, homes, cars, and bodies prove hopelessly inadequate. We are not good at cold.

The view from inside the house is deceiving: The frigid air holds little moisture and leaves no frost; the low-angled sun and cloudless sky give the appearance of an early summer morning. There is no indication that it's anything but a beautiful day – until you go outside. Or, worse yet, out to my unheated office. Even when I'm dressed in state-of-the-art puff gear, work becomes almost impossible. Fingerless gloves allow me to hit the keyboard in 15-minute spurts before my hands seize up. I drag in the old space heater, run it on high for three hours, and find the thermometer on my desk reading a tropical 34 degrees.

To summarize: Can't work, can't pick mushrooms, can't believe the alarming rate at which the woodpile is disappearing...might as well go fishing.

In the winter months, immature resident Chinook salmon, or blackmouth, feed heavily on herring and candlefish throughout our inland sea. At times, they even chase the baitfish into protected bays where I can fish from our small, open skiff in relative comfort and safety. On especially calm, windless days, I sometimes even venture out onto the open waters of the Sound, although such expeditions are not without anxiety. The object of this pursuit, though, is worth more than any discomfort, physical or mental. Smaller than the migrating adult kings of summer, blackmouth average four to eight pounds, with a good one (at least around the Island) going 12 or 14. They are delicious, and the opportunity to eat fresh, fat-laden salmon in the dead of winter feels like a great luxury. This winter has been a bust so far. Perhaps the cold weather will trigger something, maybe move the bait in toward shore and the blackmouth along with it. Tomorrow could be the day.

I throw the last of our precious "cold weather" madrona on the fire and try to get to sleep early, but I'm filled with the same night-before-fishing anticipation I've felt since I was four years old. I lie in bed listening to the soft cadence of Stacy breathing, and stare out the window at the night sky. It's rare to see the brilliance of winter stars from beneath our usual blanket of clouds. Tonight, though, they sparkle with clarity, as cold and hard as diamonds. I watch Orion's three belt stars trace their shallow arc across treetops to the south. Each year, the trees at the edge of our woods grow ever closer to obscuring Orion's winter passage, and I wonder: When I can no longer see these stars, will I remember to miss them? One day, I will wake to find Skyla all grown up and hurtling out the door into the wider world. Shortly after, Weston will follow. I finally fall asleep reminding myself to hold on to the minutes and days, even as they slip by faster with every passing year.

Two minutes before my alarm goes off, I wake and check the treetops outlined against a starry sky. Not a hint of movement; the calm weather has held. I was half hoping the wind would give me an excuse to curl back under the covers and avoid the bitter cold. No such luck. As I climb the creaking stairs in the dark, I see light from Weston's partially opened door. When I peek in, he's sitting in the recliner, legs crossed and the big dinosaur book open on his lap. He's so engrossed in Jurassic life he doesn't even know I'm there. Skyla's room is cool and dark, her breathing deep and rhythmic. I hate to wake her. When I shake her shoulder, she frowns in her sleep, then stretches and opens her eyes.

"Hi Daddy," she says, "Are we going fishing today?"

"No," I say, feeling sudden regret, "you're going to school."

"Then why are you wearing your fishing clothes?" she asks.

"Because after I take you to school, I'm going to fish."

"I wish I could go with you."

"Me, too."

Weston comes in dragging Blue-Blue, his beloved blanket. He's clearly wide awake in spite of the dark hour. "Are we going fishing today?" he asks.

Over hot oatmeal I try to convince them (and myself) that it's too cold for little kids to go fishing. It's 16 degrees out. When I drop Skyla off at school, she hesitates outside in the dark and whispers, "I really wish I could go fishing with you today." "I know," I say. "We'll go soon." Then she lets go of my hand and disappears into the brightly lit crowd of first-graders, calling happy greetings to her friends.

At the boat ramp, I back the trailer down to the water's edge, hop out, and remove the transom straps. Two bundled-up old salts working on various projects around the dock wave, and we exchange the obligatory "Cold enough for ya?" and "Frickin' freezing." They appear surprised to see someone going fishing, and their questioning stares fill me with doubt. Maybe it is crazy to be trying to fish in this weather.

I back the trailer into the water and stand on the tongue to push the boat free. It won't budge. I push harder. Nothing. I try a different angle. I strain and heave until veins bulge in my forehead and the chronic pinched nerve in my shoulder starts sending my back into spasm. When I peer over the bow to see if anyone's witnessing this pathetic struggle, the old guys are looking right at me, puzzled by my predicament. "Boat's frozen to the trailer," I shout and return to my efforts. "You might try unhooking the winch strap on the bow there," one of them says. That thing two inches in front of my nose that holds the boat on the trailer? Right.

Once the boat's free and in the water, things get a little better. But only a little. The bowline is frozen into a solid block and I have to rummage around and find another line. Then the motor won't start. The battery seems okay, but I'm worried about running it down with too many attempts. I pump the fuel line and try again. It turns over, chugs a few times and quits. I turn the key yet again, with the same results. Over my shoulder, I can feel my audience watching, and I have a powerful urge to put the boat back on the trailer and skulk home. I twist the throttle wide open and return it to the start position. One more shot. The motor coughs, pops, sputters...and a chunk of ice shoots out of the cooling indicator tube, followed by a steady stream of water and a smooth, purring idle.

I cast off and a sudden, remarkable sense of freedom sweeps over me. What's that Thoreau quote about leaving your troubles behind? I'm there. I'm also strangely...warm. In the summer, it can be 90 degrees on land and the minute you're in a boat on the Sound, you need a jacket. This must be the opposite side of the same phenomenon: The stable temperature of this huge body of water mitigates the cold, making it warmer in the boat than on land. I think I've stumbled onto some kind of important truth here. Either that, or the humiliation I just experienced raised my body temperature along with my blood pressure.

Ten feet from the dock, I lower a dodger and plastic squid into the water and I'm fishing. Even better, I'm downright toasty. I take off my gloves and outer jacket and start looking for diving birds. This time of year, when you find the big Western grebes, with their graceful, curving necks and stylishly raked black caps, you usually find bait; when you find bait, you find salmon. Sometimes, anyway. I have no idea how these birds can paddle along the surface and stay directly above a school of herring 50 feet down, but they do. And I'm more than happy to use them as markers. It gives me something to look for during what would otherwise be random trolling.

Out by the first channel buoy, I spot a dozen grebes alternately diving and sitting, so I know they're on bait. When I reach them, the depth-finder screen lights up with a huge bait ball on the bottom in 56 feet of water. But I have to be careful out here; the big Seattle car ferry is due any time now and not paying attention could be disastrous. I turn the boat and make a slow pass through the birds, my eyes glued to the fishing rod, stomach tingling with anticipation. Somewhere in the depths, hordes of frantic baitfish bounce off my line. I'm ready to leap out of my seat, but nothing happens. When I clear the far side of the bait, I can't believe I haven't hooked a fish.

I make a sharp turn and come back through the bait again, and this time, the rod tip dips, then bounces down. Fish on! I grab the rod out of the holder, set the hook, and reel up slack in a frenzy, finally getting tight to...a little less resistance than I want. A lot less, actually. In fact, the slow trolling speed (about 2½ miles per hour) planes the fish up to the surface, where I see it's a king salmon all right – about nine inches long. Shaker. Kings less than the legal 22-inch size limit are referred to as "shakers" for their high-frequency movement when hooked. I lean over the side and release the tiny fish with a sharp twist of the hook. Within minutes, I'm fishing again, but a startling horn blast warns me that the ferry is bearing down, and I have to reel up fast to get out of the ship's way. When it's passed, I return to where I was fishing, but the bait is gone.

The day is flat-out gorgeous. No wind, and the mirrored surface of the Sound reflects a cloudless, silver-blue sky in every direction. An old-timer I know would call it a hundred dollar day, an expression that, having been outpaced by inflation, is now frequently misinterpreted as sarcasm.

I troll out of the harbor and down the shoreline to the south, adjusting my fishing gear to stay near the bottom as the shoal falls away into deep water. When I clear the point where the old creosote plant once stood, my eyes are drawn east across the open Sound and up, past the Seattle skyline, past the dark, fir-shrouded foothills, up and up to the staggering sight of Mount Rainier towering above the landscape. It's always a surprise seeing Rainier. Most of the time our local volcano remains hidden by clouds and you forget it's there. When the skies clear, it seems too tall and impossibly close to be real. The brain struggles to accept the massive shape, the glaciated flanks, the flying-saucer lenticular cloud cap hovering above the summit.

Seeing Rainier reminds me to turn and look back to the west, where the black, forested ridges of the Island and, beyond them, the Kitsap Peninsula provide a foundation for the snowy, shark-tooth alpine peaks of the Olympics. Like Rainier, they seem much too close and steep to be real. You have to consciously adjust the angle of your neck to see their tops.

No sign of grebes or bait or fish, but it hardly matters. It's such a rare pleasure to be outside and fishing in comfort – in a December cold snap, no less – that at least for the moment, I am content. I take off my heavy puff jacket and enjoy the soft breeze created by the walking-speed pace of the boat.

A young, terrier-sized harbor seal appears, swimming along in the prop wash, matching my speed with very little effort. He's close enough that I can see his whiskers against dappled gray fur and the long eyelashes framing liquid black eyes. I fight the impulse to anthropomorphize. He is not "keeping me company" or being "friendly." I know better. No matter how cute, this is the enemy. And I know what he's up to...he's waiting for me to hook a fish so he can steal it off my line, an increasingly common occurrence on the Sound. If it were summer, when my sole focus is to put salmon in the freezer, I would be throwing sinkers, hex nuts, and anything else I could grab to scare him away. But this is winter, and for now, I can live with his presence. As long he's there, I won't land a fish. Not that I'm hooking any anyway. What the heck, it's kind of nice having a little "company." After an extended time following along at a leisurely pace, the seal runs out of patience, and with a "disdainful" snort swims off for more productive hunting grounds.

Hours pass, and as usual, time warps. One minute I'm struggling to launch the boat, and the next I look up to see the sun dipping into the southwestern horizon. My day has evaporated into cold, dry air. It's been a good one, calm and relaxing, and though fishless, I feel refreshed. I stow my gear and run for the harbor, anxious now to get home, clean the boat, play with the kids, and slide back into the routines of home.

Just outside the harbor I enter into a familiar debate with myself. Should I put the gear back down and fish my way in? I've caught a lot of fish here on tides like this one. But it would be smart to get home early enough to back the boat down the driveway and wash it in daylight. On the other hand, I'm already here...

Without much conviction, I put the gear back in the water and begin a slow troll toward the ramp. I look to make sure the ferry is still at the dock loading cars, and when I glance back at the rod, it bounces, and then pulls down in a deep bend. Line peels off the reel. I pull back and feel solid resistance. The fish arcs across the narrow channel, then powers to the top, shooting along the surface with its back half out of the water like a torpedo. Remembering my "friend" the seal, I scan the water nervously and apply maximum pressure. When the fish slows, I put the motor in neutral and drift. Now I just need to make sure it's a hatchery fish, marked by a missing adipose fin, before putting it in the boat. If it's a wild fish, with fin intact, I will release it, but I'm having a hell of a time determining which it is through the glare. The fish rolls and veers under the boat. When it surfaces again, it's downlight, and I can see the empty place on the wrist of the tail where an adipose fin should be. I scoop the fish into the net and bring it aboard.

And what a fish it is: 12 pounds of luminous chrome king salmon, thick through the belly and shoulders, a deep purple sheen along the back. The metallic, grassy scent of king salmon fills the air. The fish thrashes, and I fumble around for the old hammer handle and deliver a sharp, clean blow to its head. It shakes once and relaxes, lying still. Quickly now, while its heart still beats with residual impulse, I put the fish in the fish box, tilted head down, and cut the gills to bleed it.

I wipe down the floorboards and fill out my salmon tag with shaking hands. Because it's calm and pleasant on the water, I shut off the motor and clean the fish in the boat. I make a shallow cut up the center of the belly to a point just below the gills, being careful not to puncture the entrails (digestive juices and bile can taint the meat) or cut myself. Next I run the knife inside the gill plates, severing the gills at the base of the tongue. When I pull, it all comes out in one long, dripping mass, which goes into a bucket for future crab bait. I pause to examine the stomach contents and find seven finger-sized herring in various states of digestion. A long slice on either side of the dark kidney, which runs along the backbone, a quick scrape with a spoon, and I'm done. I rinse the fish quickly over the side, keeping a sharp eye out for the seal, and put it back in the box. This fish, with its exceptionally thick belly walls and firm, icy flesh, will be magnificent eating, a winter meal the whole family craves.

After it has spent the requisite day or two in the fridge to develop optimum flavor and texture, I will cut inch-thick steaks vertically from the center of one fillet and salt them *shioyaki* style. Although there's enough of this fish to provide several dinners, we'll allow ourselves only one. The fact is, these resident kings, which live their whole lives within the confines of Puget Sound, are polluted. A century of heavy industry has sent PCBs, mercury, and various other chemicals up the food chain, collecting most prominently in the fat and flesh of apex predators from king salmon to orcas to...us. The health department says the benefits of eating fish (protein, omega-3 fatty acids, etc.) outweigh the hazards, but adds that resident Chinook salmon should not be consumed more than once a month.

So...we'll err on the safe side and celebrate with one perfect meal of fresh winter blackmouth. The rest will be stripped of fat, skin, and dark meat (where a majority of the chemicals end up), and then brined, lightly smoked, and pressure canned for a special treat in the months to come. The shelf-stable canned salmon is healthier for us and frees up valuable freezer space. Still, the whole chemical issue tarnishes some of our pleasure, and forces us to consider the effects of human activities on the food chain. Health department consumption advisories do cause some anxiety in our household, but I wonder whether the antibiotics, growth hormones, and pesticides found in commercial meat and produce are any better for us? How about the chemical preservatives and artificial colorings in processed food?

Back at the ramp, I wave to the puttering old salts with a renewed confidence, based, I admit, on the pure luck of having a fish in the boat. I am now a fisherman, a provider of food, a skilled boatman. That I load the boat on the trailer without incident enhances my feeling of competence. It's been a perfect day. The water was calm, I've been warm for hours, and there's a fat winter king in the fish box.

It's surprising how little time it takes for that sense of perfection to vanish. Thirty minutes, to be exact. Or the time it takes, in the process of washing the boat, to encase the entire boat, trailer, and driveway in a sheet of clear ice, and then slip on said ice, bark my shin on the trailer tongue, and fall to the ground in a slow-motion, wildly flailing descent. From this new, ground-level perspective, I notice that it has suddenly gotten very dark and I am, once again, freezing.

The porch light flickers on. Skyla comes barreling out into the dusk, shouting "Dad! What are you doing down there? Did you catch anyth...is that ice?" Weston follows her and they slide across the driveway, laughing and chasing each other. Weston puts his hands on the hull of the boat, and for reasons known only to him licks the frozen metal. "It'th a boat popthicle," he announces before peeling his tongue from the ice. My day edges back toward perfect.

Skyla spots the fish box on the ground and they run to it. "Dad, did you get a blackmouth?" Weston asks. Skyla pries the lid open. "You did!" she says. I crouch down with them to examine the fish. They feel its teeth, extend the fins and study the pearlescent scales that come off onto their hands. "Can we eat it tonight for dinner?" Skyla asks. I know it will taste better tomorrow or the next day, that patience will be rewarded if we can wait. But looking at her now, I understand that she doesn't want to wait. Actually, neither do I. "Sure," I say, "let's eat it tonight."

CONVERSATION WITH STACY

Me: *Aaaaaaaaaaahhh!* We're going to run out of wood
by February!

Stacy: Calm down. You say that every year.

Me: But this year I mean it.

Stacy: You say *that* every year too.

Me: Yeah, and what happens?

Stacy: You end up finding some dry logs somewhere and
we're fine.

Me: And what if I don't?

Stacy: I'm not worried about it. (*Throws two more logs into
the woodstove*)

Me: Hey, hey...take it easy. Didn't you hear what I said?

Stacy: I heard you, but I'm still not worried. Something'll turn
up when we need it.

Me: Yeah, only through a lot of effort and anxiety on my part.

Stacy: See? Nothing to worry about.

FIREWOOD IV: PRODUCTION

The stove is eating through our woodpile like a starving beaver. My distress grows with each trip to the shed as I watch formerly towering stacks of dry wood dwindle away. After weeks of bitterly cold rain, a severe snowstorm blanketed the region, followed by a cold snap with temperatures into the teens. We've been burning the stove around the clock. According to the weather service, the future holds more of the same. "The good news," I report to Stacy, with forced optimism, "is that we've only burned half our wood." Then, under my breath, "The bad news is, we're less than a third of the way through winter."

Our current wood production, which we won't burn until *next* winter, is off to a promising start. Piles of rounds from a big fall cutting season line the yard, and each morning, I grab the maul and split a few before starting work. On weekends, the kids and I stack the split wood in crisscross patterns to dry. If it gets windy and more trees come down, I'll still go out and cut, but for the most part, wintertime is splitting season.

I have plenty of incentive to split wood before work. The average winter temperature in my unheated office hovers around forty degrees, and twice this month it has dropped enough that I had to break ice stalagmites from the sink. A quick chopping session gets the blood moving before I sit down at my desk. Maybe you've heard the old saying about firewood warming you twice – when you split it and when you burn it? In my experience, it's more like five times: cutting, hauling, splitting, stacking, and carrying it to the house all produce more than a little body heat. Add in the actual burning, and we're up to six. That's a lot of warmth from one log.

A friend (and fellow wood rat) once wondered aloud why people spend money on both presplit cordwood delivery and gym memberships. I said it must save them time, and he pointed out that going to the gym isn't without impact on the day planner. True. On the other hand, guys who spend time in the gym tend to look better without shirts on than I do. And their workouts carry significantly less risk of ending with a hand-forged Scandinavian ax head imbedded in their shins. I'm okay with that. I just have to work carefully and keep my shirt on.

Right now, though, I'm concerned with *this* year's wood supply. A convergence of factors – the cold weather, my desire to have a warmer house (which seems to be increasing as I get older) and fishing too much last year – has created something of an inventory shortfall. Of course, it's not like we're going to freeze. We can always crank up the furnace, which we're already doing at a rate directly proportional to the woodpile shrinkage, but it feels like cheating. More importantly, running the furnace 24/7 would put a dent in our bank account I'm not sure we could repair. Somehow, I'm going to have to find that rarest of winter commodities in our dripping forest: dry, ready-to-burn trees. I need a miracle.

A month ago, my friend Travis, in the process of showing off his new, state-of-the-art, all-steel peavey (a lever-and–swinging hook contraption for moving logs around), casually mentioned that he might know where to find some dry timber. I let it pass, not wanting to sound too eager and unsure of his firewood expertise. For all I knew, he could be a greenwood burner. I might have been a little jealous of the gleaming peavey, too. Then the conversation got a little more serious. We debated the merits of full-skip chain-saw chains (fewer cutting teeth, higher speed, more danger) and moved on to a maul vs. wedge discussion. Finally, I asked, "What do you think of hemlock?" He wrinkled his nose in disgust. "Hate it," he declared. Okay, then.

"So, about that dry wood..." I asked, trying to sound as if I could take it or leave it. "Yeah," he said, "I think it's good to burn now, but it's ugly. I mean, big, old gnarly firs that've been down for three years. In a huge pile." Then he brightened: "We'll definitely need the peavey." He said he'd call when he was ready, but I didn't hold my breath.

Travis calls just as I'm loading the woodstove and fighting to tamp down my desperation over our meager wood supply. I'm still skeptical of finding dry wood on the ground anywhere in western Washington, but I grab my cutting gear and drive to the site through a light flurry of snow.

I can see that he was right about at least one thing: It's ugly. And dangerous. Travis is standing on the road when I arrive, looking up at a logjam of enormous second-growth fir trees, each trunk held off the ground by others and clearly under tension in multiple directions. No wonder nobody's claimed them.

We walk around the pile several times, trying to figure out the angles and pressure points. Gradually, a strategy for dismantling the logjam becomes clear, like the solution to a complicated equation. First, using a measuring stick and pruning saw, we mark 16-inch lengths along all the exposed logs. Then I climb up to the top of the pile with a light chain saw to cut away limbs while Travis clears space at ground level with his big saw. When the top trees are free of branches, we use the peavey to roll them down off the pile and into cutting position.

Snow keeps falling, and soon we're working in a wonderland of white light and muffled sound. It's a rare cold, dry snow, a welcome relief from the usual muddy quagmire of winter cutting. The rounds are monstrous, some of them so thick that the 24-inch saw bar can't reach all the way through, and each 16-inch length hits the ground with a thud we can feel through our boot soles. We're going to have to quarter the rounds in place just to move them. I start in with the maul and wedges, first splitting each round in half, then in half again. If I bend my legs and hug each quarter-round to my chest, I can just barely stand and stagger up to the road with it.

Some miraculous combination of how the logs were suspended above the wet ground and their intact bark has kept the wood dry and perfectly cured. I tap two smaller pieces together and the hollow, ringing sound confirms our hopes. You couldn't get better firewood if you dried it in a kiln. I feel like we've struck gold. "You were right, Travis," I say. "This is unbelievable." He could easily say, "I told you so," but he just shrugs, flips his face shield down, and goes back to cutting.

After I wrestle a particularly heavy quarter round onto the tailgate, I lean over, sweat dripping onto my glasses and my lower back going numb. My breath comes in ragged jets of steam, the last few puffs drifting in the still air like small, individual clouds. I'm beat. While I try to recover, I count growth rings on the quarter-round, losing track after 100, with many more to go. This tree somehow survived the rise and fall of the sawmill in Blakeley Harbor (once the largest in the country) and another at Port Madison; the clearing of land for strawberry farms in the early twentieth century; and, finally, the more recent clearing for the Island's newest product, suburban sprawl. It's strange to think of everything this old tree lived through, only to come down on a windy day three years ago.

There's still the small matter of getting the wood home. I strap the kid seats to the roof to make more space, then fill the cargo area, backseat, and shotgun seat to the ceiling. With night falling, I'm only going to get one trip in today, so I want to make it count. One last, massive quarter round goes on my lap, and after a quick run-through to make sure I can still steer and work the gearshift, I shout goodbye to Travis and pull onto the road. The car smells like a Christmas tree farm.

No matter how dry I think the wood might be, I won't know for sure until it's in the stove. And, like a kid with a new toy, I can't wait to try it out. I turn the floodlights on in our driveway, unload the quarter rounds, and get to work. Splitting wood turns out to be a lot more fun when I'm going to burn it in 15 minutes instead of 15 months. Skyla and Weston come outside to watch, and when I ask them to start carrying wood to the house, they disappear into the backyard.

The kids come back a minute later, dragging their bright orange plastic sled through two inches of snow. Great idea! Why didn't I think of it? I guess you have to live farther north – or possess the open mind of a child – to see how snow might work to your advantage. We load the clean, freshly split wood into the sled and they mush it to the house with ease.

Stacy already has a pile of hot, glowing coals going in the stove. She puts in two pieces of the new wood, shuts the door and opens the air intake. In less than 30 seconds, the stove fills with flames. I open the door to listen for hissing steam but hear only crackling fire and the occasional snap and pop. A sense of satisfaction completely out of proportion to the simple act of cutting wood and burning it settles over me.

Do we have enough to last through the winter? I doubt it. But the house is warm, the stove's roaring, and it's almost time for dinner. That seems like plenty for now.

CRAB FOR CHRISTMAS

It's the day before Christmas Eve and I'm alone in the boat off the south end of the Island, miles from where we usually set our pots. I don't know if there are any crabs here, or for that matter, where to start looking. The calm-weather forecast is holding up, though, so I'm making short sets and moving the pots around, searching for signs of life in unfamiliar waters.

My plan is to soak the pots overnight, hope the weather holds, and come back with the kids in the morning to harvest our Christmas Eve dinner. Of course, as with most of my plans, there are complicating factors: We'll need to have the boat back on the trailer by 11:00 a.m. so we can drive to the ferry dock and pick up my mom and her husband, Carey, who are coming from California for the holidays. Which is why I'm crabbing here. It's the only place close enough to town that we can make our pickup time.

When Skyla was born, my mom decided distance wasn't going to keep her from a close relationship with her granddaughter. For seven years, she has come the 1,000 miles from her home nearly once a month to be here with Skyla and, later, Weston. My mom doesn't mess around, either. She comes to work. Within minutes of her arrival, she jumps into our family routine, always quick to change a diaper (in the early days), wash dishes, or indulge the kids with pure, undivided attention. They call her Bachi, Skyla's first pronunciation of the Japanese word for grandmother, *obachan*. Carey goes by Jichi, for *jichan*, or grandfather. Last month, they were in New York to help my brother and Sarah after Nora was born, making this the longest time between visits we've ever had. The kids and I agree: Fresh winter crab would be the best way to celebrate their arrival.

I set a string of four pots, and when the final one goes in, I circle back to check the first. After pulling 80 feet of line into the boat, I look over the gunwale through 15 feet of clear winter water to see the mottled, dark red backs of rock crabs filling the pot. Not a single Dungeness. I'm going to have to move my pots. I reach inside to release the unwanted rock crabs, but in my haste – I'm already thinking of where to try next – I get careless. The last crab somehow reaches back with a meaty pincer, grabs my thumb, and crushes down. The pain is shocking. I flail around the boat, shouting and hopping up and down until the crab finally releases its grip and splashes into the water. To anyone observing, I'm sure it's the best thing they'll see all day.

I am four years old, poking at a bucket full of crawdads with a stick. It's a warm autumn afternoon and my mom and dad are both there on the riverbank with me. We are excited about the unexpected bonanza – a deer carcass in shallow water, covered with crawdads. My dad is catching them and dropping them in the bucket. He tells me to be careful, but I ignore him, completely absorbed by the scuttling creatures and their ominous claws. By my four-year-old calculations, the stick is plenty long enough. Then the biggest crawdad in the bucket reaches up with astonishing speed and clamps onto my tiny finger...

As I motor south in search of a better spot, the memory fades, but lingers in the back of my mind. I distractedly drop two pots just off the beach in open water, handling the lines gingerly with my sore thumb. Then, lacking any real strategy and running out of daylight,

I dump the other two pots in a protected bay farther to the south. I cross my fingers and hope I'm lucky.

In the morning, a stiff breeze rustles through the ferns and huckleberry shrubs outside the house. So much for the forecast. Man plans, Mother Nature laughs. But our outing still looks doable. Marginal, but doable. The kids are already up, bouncing through the house singing "Jingle Bells" as they search for mittens and hats. Weston asks if he can have a candy cane to bring in the boat. Skyla wants to know if I'm wearing my lucky fishing necklace. There's way too much excitement to bail. Might as well hook up the boat and go take a look.

I am seven years old, on a picnic at the lake with my parents. I want to fish so badly I can't sit still through lunch; each bite takes an eternity to chew and swallow. My eyes do not leave the water. Finally, I am casting the new yellow bass plug I ordered from Herter's and paid for with allowance money. After a hundred, a thousand, a million casts into this unlikely-looking water, the lure seems to pull back, and miraculously, a three-pound smallmouth bass leaps into the air. "Mom! Dad!" I shout, "I got one!"

Beyond the riffled surface of the harbor, a small wind chop is building outside. Less than ideal, but safe – at least for the time being. We only need to run about a mile down the beach in open water to the first pots, then into the sheltered bay for the others. We'll have to go more slowly than I planned, but I think we'll have just enough time to pull the pots and make it back to pick up the grandparents.

We hit the bigger stuff just outside the last channel marker, and I cut back to half throttle. I worry the pounding might be too much for the kids, but after a few minutes to adjust, they're having a great time. Two pairs of small, mittened hands grip the bow rail as they lean into the wind, smiling. I realize my jaw has been clenched tight since we launched, and it feels good to let it relax.

Above us, a swollen cloud cover hangs almost low enough to touch. Below, the water churns and swirls, reflecting the gunmetal sky. It's tough to tell whether the spray speckling my glasses is rain or saltwater. To the west, at the base of dark, fir-covered hills, buttery light pours from the windows of beach houses, and Christmas lights twinkle on the eaves. A quarter mile offshore, the wind still carries a hint of wood smoke.

I am 11 years old. It's the week before Christmas, my parents are divorced, and I have spent an entire year trying without success to catch a steelhead. All I want – at least that I can articulate – is a steelhead. Desperate to help her fish-crazed son, my mom has called Andy Landforce, the legendary Oregon guide, for help. And now, he is rowing his old wooden drift boat, I am standing in the bow, and I have a fish on. A steelhead. I am terrified of losing it. When the fish surges away and runs far downstream, my heart pounds like it's going to explode.

I can't find the first set of pots. We zigzag around the area where I thought I dropped them: 110 feet of water off the house with the green roof. But no buoys. Time ticks away; my internal pressure builds. Maybe the tide dragged them off, maybe someone else picked them up.

"There it is! Way over there," Skyla shouts, pointing to a distant speck of orange, the flag marker on top of our pot buoy. It was the *other* house with a green roof.

We pull alongside the buoy, and Skyla reaches over the portside bow, grabs the buoy pole and passes it back to Weston, who passes it to me. I'm happy to see they remember our routine from last summer, and everything goes smoothly, in spite of the boat's heaving motion. I pull a suspiciously light pot to the surface and it comes over the side empty. Nada. Zip. Zero. Three sets of shoulders slump. But when I open the pot door to get rid of the bait, both kids brighten. "Dad, can I throw the salmon head over the side?" Weston asks. "I'll throw the tail and skeleton," Skyla says. They proceed with gusto, and I remind myself of the same old lesson, *The path is the goal.*

Our second pot comes up with more resistance, and I'm cautiously hopeful when my arms and back start burning with exertion. The kids are watching me, trying to gauge my effort as an indicator of what might be in the pot. When most of the line is in the boat, they crouch along the gunwale and peer into the water, watching and waiting.

"I see it, Daddy, I see it," Skyla hollers.

"Anything in it?" I ask between labored breaths.

"Yeah," she says, "It's...it's a...YAAAAAAAY! We got a humongous starfish! And it's *purple!*"

I take a deep breath and tell myself again: *The path. It's always the path.*

The kids pull the giant sunflower star from the pot, and it takes both of them to lift it, water streaming down their arms. They shed their soaked mittens to feel its rough surface and giggle when hundreds of tiny suction feet pull at their skin. I take a picture of them holding up their prize, beaming with excitement beneath a darkening sky.

I glance at my watch. We have 45 minutes to find and pull the remaining pots, get them lashed down safely, and make it back to the ramp. At half throttle, assuming the building chop doesn't slow us down even more, it's going to be tight. At least we'll have the wind behind us on the way back; we can run faster in following seas.

When we turn into the lee of Restoration Point, the wind falls out and the surface of the small bay flattens to a silvery sheen. We can make up some time here, and I already see our buoys in the calm water ahead. I am focused on making a beeline to the pots when Weston shouts, "Dad, stop!" I cut the throttle to see what the problem is.

"Look over there," he says, "Santa Claus is crabbing, too!" There's another boat in the bay. It's a big old Glasply, the classic workhorse boat of Puget Sound, and sure enough, standing in the back at an electric pot puller is a big man with a white beard wearing a fur-trimmed red velvet hat. The kind of Santa hat you can buy at the drugstore for $2.99...or have made by elves in your workshop at the North Pole. We wave and the man smiles, waves back, and yells, "Ho, ho, ho!"

Our second set of pots lies in 75 feet of water about halfway into the bay. We can work easily here, protected from the wind and current of the open Sound. I'm not fooled, though. On the ridge to the south, big firs bend and sway, and behind us the waves are starting to turn white on top.

I charge up to the buoy, throw the motor into neutral, and we get to work. The kids pass the flag back and I start hand-over-handing the line as fast as I can. It feels heavy, but with the giant starfish fresh in my memory, I try not to get too excited. Skyla sees it first. "Crabs!" she says. "I see crabs in the pot!" And when it gets closer to the surface, "Dungies, too! Keepers!"

Success. We haul the pot – loaded with pale-purple Dungeness crabs – into the boat. "Oh, those are dandies!" Weston says. We sort through the pile, each kid taking turns releasing the undersize and female crabs, being extra careful to avoid the pincers. When the pot's clear, we have four big, hard-shelled keepers in the bucket. Not the mother lode, but a good score. And we know that these winter crabs will be packed with firm, sweet flesh, more succulent and cleaner tasting than the ones we get in summer. They will make a special dinner.

The last pot yields three more keepers. We're done. We're also late. I pour each kid a cup of hot apple cider from the thermos, then quickly stack the pots and tie them down for the rough ride home. The last thing we want is loose pots flying around a bucking boat. Skyla and Weston sip their drinks and crouch around the bucket of crabs, poking at them cautiously. "Be careful," I say. "One might reach up and grab you." I have become my father.

"Okay, hold on tight now!" I shout as we head out into the open water. The wind came up while we were in the bay, packing the steep waves closer together than I'd like. I trim the motor to bring the bow up, and we climb the back of each wave at half throttle, then coast down the front at near idle, plunging into the troughs. Water sloshes out of the crab bucket. The ferry is behind schedule, too, just coming across from Seattle, throwing white spray to both sides, lumbering toward the Island.

We'll take it slow, and if we're late, we're late. If it gets too rough, I can always wait for the ferry to pass us and poach the flat wake it leaves behind. For now, I just need to concentrate and pick my way through the chop. A hypnotic rhythm to the driving sets in – throttle up, back off, coast down, gun it back up again. It's like driving a car at night in a blizzard, when everything disappears but the streaking snowflakes lit by headlights. It's just waves now, one after another, rolling up and under us.

The kids are in the bow, hands clenched tight to the rail and wind in their faces, laughing as they leap in time to the pounding of the boat. Skyla's hair streams out behind her, and Weston shrieks with delight each time we surf down into the trough. I catch myself hoping that this might become one of their childhood memories.

I can see my dad coming across the pasture with a gunnysack full of salmon over his shoulder. It's raining hard. We are warm and dry inside the car, my mom reading while I stare through rain-streaked windows, waiting. I couldn't fish with him because the weather was too much for a little kid, and now my eyes feel thick and tired from crying earlier. When he opens the door, I smell rain, wet wool, and salmon. I want to see the fish, but I don't have my shoes on. He carries me outside and we look at the big, bright silvers lying in the trunk.

Did it occur to my father, in what must have been October 1969, as he walked back from fishing in the rain, that this moment would become one of my enduring memories? That 40 years later, the smell of wet wool would always bring this day back? What about the time when I was five and we walked to the mailbox to find a job offer waiting, and he swung me through the air with both hands, smiling at our bright future? Did he know that would stay with me?

My mom is picking persimmons in the backyard of a new house. She's impossibly young, her long black hair held back with a bandanna, taking a break from unpacking our new life in a new state. The sun here feels hot and unfamiliar. I hold the basket for her, trying to help. "Go ahead," she says, "try one." When I bite into the smooth, bright orange persimmon, I am surprised by its astringency.

There must have been other, more significant moments my parents hoped I would remember. But they've somehow slipped from my consciousness and disappeared.

Across the Sound, I can see whitecaps building and a dark wall of rain closing in. The storm is bearing down fast. As we make the turn into the calm waters of the harbor, I look at the kids leaping and laughing in the bow and wonder, Will something of this day become a part of their future selves? The bite of cold winter air on their hands, a bucket full of crabs in the boat, the anticipation of Christmas with their grandparents...will they remember it forever? I know I will.

GRATITUDE

This book, and for that matter, the life we're so fortunate to lead, would not be possible without the help of many. Thanks, first of all, to my mom and dad for their constant encouragement of their fish-obsessed boy, and for the lessons necessary to finding happiness. And to Stacy, my love, supportive and optimistic, renowned for inappropriate footwear, gung-ho, game, and the toughest person I know.

Also, a special thank-you to Mike and Nancy for unwavering support over many years.

In all outdoor activities, knowledge is the currency of highest value, generally attained only through years of personal experience. I am lucky to have found incredible mentors throughout my life, and their teachings have shortened the learning curve for me time and again. My deep appreciation goes out to each of them: Andy Landforce, for early lessons in steelhead, bluegills, and life. Nate Mantua, for weather and conservation. Dan Sweeney for razor clams and the ocean. Mike Kinney for the ways of the river and steelhead to the fly. Bill McMillan, Yvon Chouinard, Bruce Hill, and Gerald Amos for opening my eyes. Bob Dawson for geoducks and the good old days. David Smart for Puget Sound. Neal McCulloch for chanterelles. Wes

Blauveldt for birds. Glen Urquhart for berry cultivation, pruning, and tree felling.

On the writing side, many thanks to Tom McGuane, Dave Guterson, Tim Pask, Steve Zaro, Marc Bale, Vincent Stanley, John Larison, and Ted Leeson for inspiration, encouragement, and wisdom. And to my brother, Adrian, for lighting the path and setting the bar so damn high.

I am proud to call each of you mentor, friend, and, with utmost respect, *sensei*.

Much gratitude, also, to my agent, Valerie Borchardt, whose patient guidance cured my addiction to industrial-strength antacids. To Susan Bell, whose skillfull editing gives my work the illusion of literacy. And to Nikki McClure, for the beautiful paper cuts that bring life to these stories. I also want to thank Vincent Stanley again here, along with the rest of the crew at Patagonia, for putting so much care into this book.

But above all, I am thankful for the teachers from whom I continue to learn the most, Skyla and Weston. The main lesson? That maybe process is more important than production, that stopping to watch birds, smell flowers, and splash in puddles is more fun than simply making a haul. I think it's rubbing off on me. I may not be ready to say the path is the only goal, but I now know it's worth enjoying along the way.

ABOUT THE AUTHOR

Dylan Tomine, formerly a fly fishing guide, is now a writer, conservation advocate, blueberry farmer and father, not necessarily in that order. His work has appeared in *The Flyfish Journal*, *The Drake*, *Golfweek*, *The New York Times* and numerous other publications. He lives with his family on an island in Puget Sound.

www.dylantomine.com.

ABOUT THE ILLUSTRATOR

Nikki McClure is known for her painstakingly intricate and beautiful paper cuts. Armed with an X-acto knife, she cuts her images from a single sheet of paper and creates a bold language that translates the complex poetry of motherhood, nature, and activism into a simple and endearing picture. Nikki's images exude a positivity that revolves around community, sustenance, parenting, and appreciating both the urban and rural landscape, undoubtedly influenced by her home in Olympia, WA. She regularly produces her own posters, books, cards, t-shirts and a beloved yearly calendar. She is a self-taught artist who has been making paper-cuts since 1996.

www.nikkimcclure.com.

THE RESPONSIBLE COMPANY

WHAT WE'VE LEARNED FROM PATAGONIA'S FIRST 40 YEARS

YVON CHOUINARD & VINCENT STANLEY

THE RESPONSIBLE COMPANY

In *The Responsible Company*, Yvon Chouinard, founder and owner of Patagonia, and Vincent Stanley, co-editor of its *Footprint Chronicles*, draw on their 40 years' experience at Patagonia – and knowledge of current efforts by other companies – to articulate the elements of responsible business for our time.

Featured on *Fortune's* cover in 2007 as "the coolest company on the planet," Patagonia has earned a reputation for its ground-breaking environmental practices as well as for the quality of its clothes. In *The Responsible Company*, Chouinard and Stanley recount how the company and its culture gained the confidence—step-by-step and misstep—to make its work progressively more responsible, and to ultimately share its discoveries with companies as large as Wal-Mart and as small as the corner bakery.

The Responsible Company shows companies how to thread their way through economic sea change and slow the drift toward ecological bankruptcy. Its advice is simple but powerful: reduce your environmental footprint (and its skyrocketing cost), make legitimate products that last, reclaim deep knowledge of your business and its supply chain to make the most of opportunities in the years to come, and earn the trust (and business) you'll need by treating your workers, customers and communities with respect.

ISBN 978-09801227-8-7
$19.95

PADDLING NORTH
by Audrey Sutherland

PADDLING NORTH

In a tale remarkable for its quiet confidence and acute natural observation, the author of *Paddling Hawaii* begins with her decision, at age 60, to undertake a solo, summer-long voyage along the southeast coast of Alaska in an inflatable kayak.

Paddling North is a compilation of Sutherland's first two (of over 20) such annual trips and her day-by-day travels through the Inside Passage from Ketchikan to Skagway. With illustrations and the author's recipes.

ISBN 978-0-9801227-5-6
$22.95

THE VOYAGE OF THE CORMORANT

CHRISTIAN BEAMISH

THE VOYAGE OF THE *CORMORANT*

The author, a former editor at *The Surfer's Journal*, envisioned a low-tech, self-reliant exploration for surf along the coast of North America, using primarily clothes and instruments available to his ancestors, and a boat he would build by hand in his garage. How the vision met reality – and how the two came to shape each other – places *Voyage of the Cormorant* in the great American tradition of tales of life at sea, and what it has to teach us.

ISBN 978-0-9801227-6-3
$24.95